MW00389419

Praise for *Your Values-Based Legacy*

"*Your Values-Based Legacy* is required reading for anyone seeking to understand what it means to build a compelling legacy. Both philosopher and practitioner, Kraemer offers powerful guidance for every point of our lives. My most valuable epiphany . . . meaningful legacy starts at the beginning and never stops—far from being an end of career phenomenon."

—Greg Case,
CEO of Aon, plc

"In this truly remarkable book, Harry Kraemer does a fabulous job of showing us how we can build a lifelong legacy of impact through the values-driven choices we make every day. He encourages us to look inward, rediscover the values modeled by our families and mentors, and use that moral foundation to create positive ripples in the world. This book is a powerful call for every one of us to embrace our potential to make an extraordinary difference."

—Hubert Joly, former Best Buy CEO;
senior lecturer Harvard Business School;
author, *The Heart of Business*

"Harry Kraemer's newest book is a must-read. Earlier in my career I thought that legacy creation was for 'later,' as being an executive and busy mom was enough for 'now.' Harry helps us learn how we can begin to set the stage throughout our lives to build the framework for the legacy we hope to leave."

—Mary Dillon, CEO of Foot Locker;
former CEO of Ulta Beauty

"Drawing from his extensive career with Baxter International and Northwestern University, Harry provides insightful guidance on honoring our past, celebrating the present, and creating a future legacy that reflects our core values. It inspires readers to take conscious steps toward creating a fulfilling and purpose-driven life—starting today. This book is a must-read for anyone looking to make a difference and leave a legacy to be proud of."

—Dr. Marshall Goldsmith,
Thinkers50 #1 Executive Coach and
New York Times best-selling author of *The Earned Life*,
*Trigger*s, and *What Got You Here Won't Get You There*

"Harry Kraemer's new book, *Your Values-Based Legacy*, not only belongs in your library at home next to his other books but more importantly it needs to be in your heart and your head. Our legacy depends on the choices we make now, and our choices for doing good for others will inspire and encourage those who come after us. And that goodness in action goes forth like a ripple effect: ever farther and ever greater."

—Rev. Francis Joseph Hoffman,
CEO of Relevant Radio

"In this deeply personal book Harry Kraemer reminds us that legacies are not what is written in obituaries but the impact we have right now, every moment, through our choices and actions, on the lives of others. I strongly recommend it to everyone who wants to live a more meaningful and impactful life."

—Daniel Diermeier, PhD
Chancellor, Vanderbilt University

"*Your Values-Based Legacy* is a testament to the wisdom, experience, and passion Harry Kraemer brings to every aspect of his life. He has a unique—and compelling—ability to weave the personal with the professional and exemplifies every aspect of the values and leadership principles he teaches in the classroom. He inspires everyone to think of their legacy and long-term impact. If you are looking for inspiration and practical guidance on how to live a life of meaning and purpose, you must spend time with Harry's *Your Values-Based Legacy*."

—Francesca Cornelli,
Dean, Northwestern University's
Kellogg School of Management

"Harry Kraemer's *Your Values-Based Legacy* provides an inspiring set of stories that demonstrate how leaders at every stage of life find their purpose and drive change throughout the world. His powerful 3Cs framework encourages each of us to weave together our connections, communities, and conscious choices into a legacy that is uniquely ours and meaningful in its impact."

—Deborah DeHaas,
CEO of Corporate Leadership Center;
former vice chair of Deloitte

YOUR VALUES-BASED LEGACY

YOUR VALUES-BASED LEGACY

"This is required reading for anyone seeking to understand what it means to build a compelling legacy."

—GREG CASE, CEO of Aon, plc

MAKING A DIFFERENCE AT **EVERY AGE** AND **PHASE OF LIFE** ➤

HARRY M. JANSEN KRAEMER, JR.

WILEY

Copyright © 2025 by John Wiley & Sons, Inc. All rights reserved, including rights for text
and data mining and training of artificial technologies or similar technologies.

Published by John Wiley & Sons, Inc., Hoboken, New Jersey.
Published simultaneously in Canada.

No part of this publication may be reproduced, stored in a retrieval system, or
transmitted in any form or by any means, electronic, mechanical, photocopying,
recording, scanning, or otherwise, except as permitted under Section 107 or 108 of the
1976 United States Copyright Act, without either the prior written permission of the
Publisher, or authorization through payment of the appropriate per-copy fee to the
Copyright Clearance Center, Inc., 222 Rosewood Drive, Danvers, MA 01923, (978)
750-8400, fax (978) 750-4470, or on the web at www.copyright.com. Requests to the
Publisher for permission should be addressed to the Permissions Department,
John Wiley & Sons, Inc., 111 River Street, Hoboken, NJ 07030, (201) 748-6011,
fax (201) 748-6008, or online at http://www.wiley.com/go/permission.

Trademarks: Wiley and the Wiley logo are trademarks or registered trademarks of John
Wiley & Sons, Inc. and/or its affiliates in the United States and other countries and may
not be used without written permission. All other trademarks are the property of their
respective owners. John Wiley & Sons, Inc. is not associated with any product or vendor
mentioned in this book.

Limit of Liability/Disclaimer of Warranty: While the publisher and author have used
their best efforts in preparing this book, they make no representations or warranties with
respect to the accuracy or completeness of the contents of this book and specifically
disclaim any implied warranties of merchantability or fitness for a particular purpose. No
warranty may be created or extended by sales representatives or written sales materials.
The advice and strategies contained herein may not be suitable for your situation. You
should consult with a professional where appropriate. Further, readers should be aware
that websites listed in this work may have changed or disappeared between when this
work was written and when it is read. Neither the publisher nor authors shall be liable for
any loss of profit or any other commercial damages, including but not limited to special,
incidental, consequential, or other damages.

For general information on our other products and services or for technical support,
please contact our Customer Care Department within the United States at (800)
762-2974, outside the United States at (317) 572-3993 or fax (317) 572-4002.

Wiley also publishes its books in a variety of electronic formats. Some content that
appears in print may not be available in electronic formats. For more information about
Wiley products, visit our web site at www.wiley.com.

Library of Congress Cataloging-in-Publication Data is Available:

ISBN: 9781394271320 (cloth)
ISBN: 9781394271337 (epub)
ISBN: 9781394271344 (epdf)

Cover Design: Paul McCarthy

SKY10084558_091624

To my two grandfathers, Farrell Grehan, a world history teacher in Queens, New York, and Dr. Harry M. Kraemer Sr., a family physician in Scranton, Pennsylvania—two amazing examples of what it means to start a legacy

To my first grandchild, Harrison Thomas Clark, whom I will encourage to continue this legacy

CONTENTS

Introduction: A Values-Based Journey   *xiii*

PART ONE
HONORING OUR PAST   1

1 OUR EARLIEST INFLUENCES   3
2 SELF-REFLECTION: THE 3CS OF OUR PAST
   TO PRESENT   25

PART TWO
CELEBRATING OUR PRESENT   47

3 THE SIGNIFICANCE OF SMALL   49
4 GROWING AT THE GRASSROOTS   77
5 FROM LOSS TO LEGACY   99
6 WHO ARE "THOSE GUYS"?   117

PART THREE
CREATING OUR FUTURE   143

7 A GLOBAL FOOTPRINT   145

8 THE CYCLE CONTINUES   165

9 WHAT THE WORLD NEEDS NOW   187

Epilogue: My Inspiration   *205*
Acknowledgments   *207*
About the Author   *209*
Appendix   *211*
Notes   *213*
Index   *223*

Values-based leadership is the journey of my life. It began during my career at Baxter International, a multibillion-dollar health care company where I spent 23 years, including 6 years as CEO. The next phase of my journey began 20 years ago, when I became a clinical professor at Northwestern University's Kellogg School of Management.

Teaching at Kellogg has led me to write three books, and now a fourth. In fact, the ideas for each of my books were generated by questions from my students. When they asked me what it takes to become a values-based leader, that discussion led to my first book, *From Values to Action: The Four Principles of Values-Based Leadership*, in which I discuss self-reflection, balance, true self-confidence, and genuine humility as being foundational to values-based leadership.

From values-based leadership the discussion moved to a values-based organization. That led to my second book, *Becoming the Best: Build a World-Class Organization Through Values-Based Leadership*. Then, right before the onset of the COVID pandemic—which, for many of us, led to both isolation and self-reflection about what matters most—a student asked me, "How do I live a values-based life?" The answer shaped my third book, *Your 168: Finding Purpose and Satisfaction in a Values-Based Life*.

After writing these three books, I thought I was finished with everything I had to say. Then Tricia Crisafulli, who has played a significant role in all three of my books, called me one evening and raised an interesting question: "Harry, how do you build a values-based legacy?" Our conversation led to this book, which you are about to read.

Initially, I expected to approach this book the way I had my first three: drawing from my teaching, the four principles, and experiences from my career and those shared by people I highly respect (many of whom are also guest speakers in my Kellogg leadership classes). As I soon found out, though, this book required a different approach. Instead of being the teacher, I became the student as I explored what it means to build a legacy. I reached out to people in my network who are doing important work to help others. They, in turn, introduced me to people in their networks, who also suggested others I should talk to. This process started with my own network, but quickly spiraled outward to many more people, including several I had never met before.

This also became the first lesson in building a values-based legacy: start where you are and with people you know and see where it leads you. Within your own network, community, and even your neighborhood, there are people and projects that are making a difference. You don't have to travel the world. You can start, literally, in your own backyard. The key word, though, is start.

Often when I speak to young professionals about legacy, they think about what they might do one day. They view it as something to put on a bucket list—when they're older and more established in their careers, after they've bought a house, after they've had children, after those children graduate from college, when they're ready to retire . . . in other words, it's something they'll do when they have more time and more money.

That's not how I view building a legacy. It's about the conscious choices you are making in your life right now. It may be a genuine commitment to show respect and kindness to others in your daily interactions with colleagues, friends, family members—or the next person you see at the coffee shop or the grocery store. You may become a dedicated volunteer with an organization in your community. You may spend a certain number of hours every week or month supporting a cause that reflects your values, your sense of purpose, and how and where you'd like to make a positive impact. In time, your vision may even become a calling. Your focus may be local or global. Whatever it is, it's all part of your legacy—on the journey we call life.

It's also important to understand what legacy is not. It has nothing to do with building your résumé. A legacy isn't about your image, your network, or your net worth. There's nothing for you to gain—except, of course, personal satisfaction. As I've heard countless times from the people interviewed for this book, as they gave of themselves—whether to a cause, a community, or an entire country—they were transformed. My good friend Stephen Isaacs, who supports and works with numerous philanthropic projects in Africa and elsewhere, said it best: "Working with people is a two-way street."

WHAT CAN ONE PERSON DO?

It's a common question—and one you may be asking yourself right now. *What can one person do?* The answer is: more than you might ever imagine.

Yes, there are many problems and challenges in our world, and solving them is beyond the capability of any one person. But when one person joins with another and then another. . . . Soon there is a critical mass of people and resources that can, indeed, lead to positive change and make a significant impact.

Just ask Andrew Youn, cofounder of One Acre Fund, a former Kellogg MBA student (you'll read about him in Chapter 7), who went to Africa with a desire to help farmers grow enough to feed their families and improve their communities. Not knowing how to do that at first, he listened and learned. Today, One Acre Fund supports more than 4 million farm families, with a goal of 10 million families. (As with all my books, I donate my proceeds, along with speaking fees and honorariums, to One Acre Fund.)

One Acre Fund is expanding its reach across Africa, but there was a time when it was only Andrew and a few people, trying to make a difference. If Andrew hadn't had this desire and acted on it, One Acre Fund would not exist. This is the difference that even one person can make in the world.

This is the essence of what it means to step up to the challenges we see around us. It's understanding that we cannot wait for someone else to solve the problems. We each can and should do something—in other words, we are the ones to do what needs to be done. Even if we don't have ample financial resources, we can give our time and talent. There is always something to contribute to others, and no effort is too small or insignificant.

When Andrew and I talked about that, we found a metaphor in a surprising place—the fable of *Stone Soup*. This well-known story goes like this: One day hungry strangers arrive in a village with nothing but an empty pot. But the people of the town refuse to give them anything to eat. Undeterred, the travelers fill their pot with water and a large stone and start to "cook" it. One by one, the villagers come to investigate this "stone soup," which the strangers promise to share. To improve the taste, a villager offers a few carrots, another gives an onion. Others come with potatoes, cabbage, a little meat. . . . Soon, that pot of soup is bubbling with tasty ingredients—and the meal is shared by all. The fable of *Stone Soup* reminds us that even a small effort, multiplied many times over, becomes significant.

Another personal inspiration for me is the poem *The Dash* by Linda Ellis (visit her site, https://lindaellis.life/the-dash-poem to read it). It tells the story of a man who delivers a eulogy at a friend's funeral. Looking at his friend's tombstone, he notes the dates: when his friend was born and when he died. What mattered most, he says, is "the dash between those years." It's the same for all of us: Our "dash"—the time we have on Earth—contains the legacy we'll leave.

Compared to the hundreds of thousands of years of human history, let alone the billions of years of our planet, our individual lives last only the blink of an eye. We are here, then we are gone. The older I get, the more I know this to be true, as time seems to be accelerating. When I look back, it feels like only 10 or 20 years ago when I was a freshman at Lawrence University—but no, it was 50 years ago. How did time pass so quickly?

No matter where we are along our life path—whether still in school, just starting careers, or well into retirement—we can discover what it means to leave a legacy. This book is meant to inspire and guide you along that journey.

In Part One, Honoring Our Past, we explore our earliest influences, those who came before us and set an example. Parents, grandparents, teachers, community members, and others provided life lessons and helped shape our lives, our purpose, and our values—in other words, what matters most. That was the legacy they gave to us, which we can carry forward. Then, engaging in self-reflection—we look back on our past to see the influences of our connections, community, and choices. These 3Cs also draw our attention to philanthropic causes and charitable activities we engaged in, no matter how big or small, in our past. These are the seeds we can sow for a lasting legacy.

In Part Two, Celebrating Our Present, we explore the examples of people who are actively making a difference, locally and globally. We learn about the "significance of small" when making a difference in our local communities and "growing at the grassroots," where what we do locally (whether in our communities or halfway around the world) relates directly to global issues.

Some legacies are born of loss, the death of a loved one or other personal tragedies. The desire to honor the memory of a loved one establishes a legacy, as you'll read with the story of a courageous, grieving mother. You'll also learn what it means to be one of those who show up and do what they can.

In Part Three, Creating Our Future, we see just how impactful a legacy can be: crossing borders, spanning continents, and bringing together generations. Here we find the story of One Acre Fund, which is not only raising millions of farm families out of poverty but also creating a legacy of local leaders who empower their communities. We'll also learn about families that seek to "pass the torch" of their legacy by establishing a foundation, ensuring that good works last beyond one generation. Finally, we'll conclude by looking at what the world needs now—and all the various people and places that can inspire and uplift us.

My hope is that, guided by this book, you'll follow your own values-based journey and build a legacy. Then one day, when you look back on your life, you will be able to say, "I tried to make a difference by doing what I could to make the world a better place." There is no greater success or satisfaction than that.

I wish you the very best on your legacy journey.

PART ONE

HONORING OUR PAST

When we reflect on our earliest influences, we see how our grandparents, parents, teachers, mentors, leaders, and role models led by example as they demonstrated the importance of caring for others. Woven into our stories of origin are our values, our purpose, and what matters most.

CHAPTER 1

OUR EARLIEST INFLUENCES

"What you leave behind is not what is engraved on stone monuments, but what is woven into the lives of others."

—Pericles

When we hear the word *legacy*, what comes to mind is often money or property. It's no wonder; Merriam-Webster's first definition of *legacy* is a bequest made in someone's will. But legacy means much more. Legacy is a treasure that we inherit and that we, in turn, can leave to others, but not in the material sense. The legacy we discuss in this book is giving of ourselves.

Grounded in a deep desire to make a difference in the world, legacy brings with it life lessons and invaluable experiences. As our values and best intentions turn into meaningful actions, legacy celebrates what is most important to us. The fruits of these efforts also live on past our lifetime.

In this chapter, we begin our exploration of legacy as part of a *continuum*—past to present, and present to future. As we contemplate where we are already making a difference, or

3

where we'd like to become more involved, we often find the imprint of our earliest influences: grandparents, parents, teachers, mentors, leaders, and others who by their example demonstrated the importance of caring for others. Thanks to these role models, legacy is part of our DNA (perhaps literally, based on the research that shows a genetic component to altruistic behavior).[1]

Genetics aside, I believe our desire to carry on a legacy is as much nurture as it is nature. In my conversations with people, particularly over the past year, I'm often struck by how their desire to give back and the activities in which they engage link them closely to early influences in their lives. Therefore, those who shaped them in the past are still playing a role in how they act in the world.

Every conversation I had with people in this book included the same question: who influenced you? The vast majority of people mentioned a family member and frequently their parents. Stephen Isaacs, a successful biomedical entrepreneur and a philanthropist who supports numerous humanitarian projects in Africa, is a perfect example. "I grew up in a single-parent home without a lot of resources," Steve explained. "But my mother was always willing to share what little we had. This was also true of my extended family—grandparents, aunts and uncles, cousins."

He recalled Sunday evening get-togethers with the family—"with rich, unhealthy food and home-based family music, all held in the haze of unfiltered cigarette smoke." Not exactly the typical idyllic scene, perhaps, but it shines brightly in Steve's memory. "The lesson from these Sunday evenings was that good times and rich experiences are based on love and togetherness and not necessarily connected to material wealth. And I then re-learned this lesson again in Africa."

Similarly, Elizabeth Goward, who manages the volunteer program for the McKenzie River Trust, a watershed protection organization in Oregon (profiled in Chapter 4), credits the influence of her mother, as well as the local community. She recalled her childhood of growing up in a family of three children raised by a single parent. "As a child, I was introduced to the YMCA, which had incredible resources to support low-income families," Elizabeth said. "I was a nonprofit baby!"

Through the YMCA and other community organizations, Elizabeth attended summer camps and spent time in the forest as a youngster, which became a lifelong influence. "It really brought out my interest and passion for the environment."

Another example is Dr. Pat Lee, president and CEO of Central Health, an Austin, Texas–based health care system (his story appears in Chapter 2), who has devoted his life to social justice and closing the gaps of health care inequities. He recalled the enduring influence of his uncle, Dr. David Lee, professor emeritus of medicine/nephrology with the David Geffen School of Medicine at University of California, Los Angeles, who believed caring for all patients was a humbling privilege. "Uncle David was the kindest person in the room. He could make you feel better about yourself, just by being there. He had that gift."

These are just some of the stories I had the privilege to hear in the writing of this book. Each example is a testimony to the enduring influence of those who came before us, to guide and inspire us in how and where we want to give back. For some people, this may be tapping the power of generational stories of giving others a helping hand. One friend of mine described how her grandparents, who had a small farm during the Depression, never turned away anyone who came to the back door asking for a meal in return for doing an odd job, such as chopping wood for the kitchen stove. Having heard these stories so much in her childhood, my friend sees it as "no surprise" that she's drawn to causes that address homelessness, poverty, and hunger in the local community.

Remembering these early influences helps us connect the dots to where and how we can be involved in the causes that resonate with us. On an emotional level, we can often see how our philanthropic efforts honor the legacy we inherited from others in our past.

MY EARLY INFLUENCES

In my own life, I can trace the roots of my legacy back to childhood. I can remember being in second grade in Catholic school and our teacher, who was a nun, passed out empty milk cartons to collect change to help feed children in developing countries. Deeply moved by images of children my age who suffered from malnutrition, I was on a mission to be the first one in the class to fill my milk carton with pennies, nickels, dimes, and the occasional quarter. Back then, empty soda bottles could be returned to the corner grocery store for a two-cent deposit and quart-sized bottles for a nickel. Soon my younger brothers and I were scouring the park for empty glass bottles to turn in for the refund. Looking back on this early influence, it's no surprise that one of the organizations I support is One Acre Fund, which seeks to eradicate poverty and hunger by increasing the productivity and profitability of farmers in Africa. (You'll be reading more about One Acre in

Chapter 7.) My support of One Acre Fund has a direct link
back to my milk carton collection days.

When I was growing up, life lessons were taught to my
three brothers, my sister, and me as part of our family values and our faith. We were expected to take responsibility,
do our best, treat others with honesty and respect, and
give to those who were less fortunate. Other kids in the
neighborhood might complain about not having a new
bicycle or only getting 25 cents for a weekly allowance. But
we didn't dare. It's not that the Kraemer kids were angels,
but we were taught to recognize how blessed we were. We
couldn't grumble about not having enough pocket money
to buy ice cream when we knew there were children halfway around the world who did not have enough food to
keep them alive.

*My parents, Harry and Patricia Kraemer, and my maternal
grandparents, Farrell and Emily Grehan.*

Me, about age two, playing with Grandpa Grehan.

When I think about specific episodes, I get quite emotional. One involved my maternal grandfather, Farrell Grehan, my mother's father. He was a world history teacher who lived in New York City—specifically, Richmond Hill, a neighborhood in Queens. I can remember visits with Grandpa Grehan when he would explain the importance of understanding the past and learning from history—all the way back to the ancient Greeks and the Roman Empire. He would talk to me about Julius Caesar, Alexander the Great, and Napoleon—and how they had focused on building their personal empires, but not on leaving legacies of a truly positive difference in the world.

One vivid memory from my younger days is when I was about seven years old and walking with Grandpa Grehan around New York's Central Park and looking at all the statues of "important people" who seemed to gaze down at me from their pedestals. Some of these statues depicted generals and other military leaders. That stirred a question in my young mind. "Grandpa," I asked one day, "why are there always wars?"

I'll never forget his reply: "Harry, since the dawn of humankind, people have killed each other. Part of it is that people don't take the time to listen to one another and don't reflect on how short of a time they're on this Earth. They're only after power and wealth—things that are very temporary."

Then Grandpa Grehan looked down at me and said, "It was only a blink of an eye ago that I was a child like you."

There I was, a young boy, looking up at my grandfather who had lived more years than I could imagine at the time (truthfully, he was just a little older than I am now). And yet, he was talking about being a child and how that felt like such a short time ago.

Of all the many discussions with Grandpa Grehan over the years, this particular conversation was a formative moment. It was the first time I began to grasp what my grandfather meant when he said, "We're here only for a very short time." This perspective is a big part of the legacy that Grandpa Grehan gave to me. Sure, I played a lot of baseball (during the summer, we started after breakfast and finished when the sun went down, with only a few breaks for meals). But from a young age, I grew up knowing that life is short, and time should not be wasted.

Dr. Harry Kraemer Sr., my paternal grandfather.

My paternal grandfather, Dr. Harry Kraemer Sr., died long before I was born. A physician in Scranton, Pennsylvania, he delivered babies for free during the Depression when his patients could not pay. Diagnosed with terminal cancer, he told his wife to destroy his accounting books because he didn't want people to have to pay after his death.

My dad was only 18 when his father died. But the stories he later told my siblings and me about him became enduring lessons, as we learned values such as giving to others in need. Money was not what mattered.

One of the biggest influences on this perspective was my father. He was a salesman, as personable a guy as you'd ever want to meet. He had several great lines (some no doubt he heard from someone else), but he sure knew how to deliver them. One of his best was, "Have you ever seen a hearse going to a cemetery with a U-Haul attached to it?"

He always got a good laugh from that one. Beyond the punchline, though, was a serious message. As Dad would say, "Most people must think they're either going to live forever or they're going to take all of this material stuff with them." It was a message I heard often, and it made an impression on me.

When I was 13 years old, I was really into cars and liked to look at the front grilles and figure out their make and model. I'd see a particular grille and know whether the car was a Ford or an Oldsmobile. Back in those days, there were big fields filled with junk cars sold for parts or scrap metal. One day, Dad and I drove past a big flatbed truck carrying a tall stack of flattened cars. Dad looked out the window and asked me, "What's the grille on the third one from the bottom?"

"That's a Mercedes," I replied.

Dad shook his head as he spoke. "You know, about 10 years ago, some guy bought that car and was so proud of it.

He'd always park it at the very end of the parking lot so no one would put a ding in the door. Didn't matter if it was raining, he'd be the farthest from the building so nothing would happen to his car. And now look, that same car is as flat as a pancake on the back of a truck."

Dad wasn't against material possessions, and neither am I. You work hard, you do well, so you want to have a nice house and a good car. It's okay to treat yourself. But we should be careful not to be possessed by our possessions. The more we cling to what we have, the less willing we are to share. If we are not careful, then giving our time, money, help, or even our ideas can feel like we're losing something.

Thanks to my family and the way I was raised, I was instilled with the importance of helping others and giving back. As my career progressed, I became chief financial officer (CFO) and then CEO and chairman of the board of Baxter International, a multibillion-dollar health care company. The higher up the ladder I climbed, the more I reminded myself constantly never to be defined by my job title or become attached to the perks of being a Fortune 100 CEO. The one person who has always kept me grounded is my wife, Julie. Whenever I'd tell her that I had been promoted, she would always say how proud she was of me, but in the next breath she'd remind me, "Harry, we're not going to change the way we live, right?" And I would assure her that we were still the same people we were back in college.

Julie and I have always been involved in our church and our community. I've taught Sunday school and did all the Boy Scout campouts, especially with my youngest son, Daniel. And I coached sports teams for all five of my children, whether soccer, softball, baseball, or basketball.

But my true calling, both personally and professionally, is being a values-based leader. I think of it this way: leadership is the ability to influence others. Values-based leadership takes it to the next level, seeking to inspire and motivate others to pursue what matters most.

After I left Baxter in 2004, I found new ways to give back as a values-based leader. It started with one of the first calls I received post-Baxter. It was from Don Jacobs, the late dean emeritus of Northwestern University's Kellogg School of Management, where I had received my MBA. Don asked me to consider teaching. I quickly agreed—I'd do anything he asked me to do—but explained that I wasn't really interested in teaching finance. For one thing, I don't have a PhD. More important, I felt a deep desire to share with students the benefits of my 23 years of real-world experiences at Baxter, including six as the CEO and chairman. This gave me a sense of mission to help new and first-time leaders understand the importance of being grounded in their values in everything they do.

Today, I am also an executive partner at Madison Dearborn, a private equity firm, and sit on the boards of several companies in our health care portfolio. Once again, this is an opportunity to provide leadership to organizations, coach and mentor executive leadership teams, and also to broaden my own experience with an open mind to learn from others.

In addition, I also serve on the board of nonprofit organizations. One of my criteria is to give to organizations that have helped inform and influence me. Given my long career in health care, in 1997, I joined the board of what was then Highland Park Hospital, which was later acquired by Evanston/Northwestern Hospital (where, coincidentally, all

make it difficult to go to a doctor's office or hospital. Other forces also affect daily life, the CDC added, including "economic policies and systems, development agenda, social norms, social policies, racism, climate change, and political systems."[6]

Desiring to bring about change in pursuit of health equity, Pat decided he would work within health care systems. This defining professional choice led him to work for a health system in Brooklyn where, as system chairman of medicine, he developed a three-year strategy to reduce a shocking statistic about the majority of the patients served: an 11-year gap in life expectancy for more than 1 million predominantly Black and Latinx people in Central Brooklyn and East New York compared to people with the same age, race, and gender in Manhattan, just a few miles away.

Tackling such a seemingly intractable problem begins with trust, Pat explained. "People need to truly believe that we, as health care professionals, have their best interests at heart." Such things as early detection of cancer and providing support to manage diabetes can improve people's health, but equally important are community resources to obtain housing, access counseling, and improve economic security.

Pat's journey continues to unfold. For example, on the day of our conversation in late 2023, he had just accepted an offer to become president and CEO of Central Health in Austin, Texas, Travis County's hospital district. Austin, a city of about 1 million people, is known for live music, arts and museums, and the University of Texas at Austin, but there is another side to the city. Austin and the surrounding Travis County area have about a 12% poverty rate.[7] As a result, from the most affluent to the poorest areas in the county, the life expectancy gap can be as much as 20 years.

This is just the kind of challenge Pat has always welcomed. "Central Health is responsible for delivering whole-person care," he added. "It starts by earning trust so we and our partners can create an effective safety net system to address the area's long-standing health disparities."

REFLECTIONS ON THE 3Cs

Connections, community, choices . . . these 3Cs run through our lives. As we look back and reflect, we see these 3Cs have helped us establish a legacy of giving to others.

By continually engaging in self-reflection, we ask ourselves where we feel drawn to make a difference, and what that might look like. In that spirit, we ask ourselves:

- *What talents do I have that I can share with others?*
- *What life experiences have prepared me to give of myself in a unique or meaningful way?*
- *Whom do I know among my connections or within my community who is currently involved in a cause or philanthropic project that speaks to me?*
- *How and where can I raise my hand and make the choice to become more involved by giving of my time and talent?*

Moving forward, we understand that the 3Cs will play a role in helping us live and build a legacy. Our connections will introduce us to opportunities. Our communities will provide guidance. And, when we are ready, our decisions will commit us to where and how to get involved.

PART TWO

CELEBRATING OUR PRESENT

Right here, right now, we can make a difference.

We do not need to wait for grandiose plans. There is significance to be found in small, but sincere, actions. At the grassroots, there are also opportunities to take on global issues in a localized way. This is how communities are formed, strengthened, and become a lasting legacy.

CHAPTER 3

THE SIGNIFICANCE OF SMALL

"Small is beautiful."

—E. F. Schumacher

Can small actions ever make a difference when the problems of the world are so enormous? It's easy to fall into this thinking. We wonder how those few cans of soup donated to the local food pantry, or a package of socks given to a clothing drive, can possibly change anything. However, if we think that only grand plans and elaborate projects have meaning, we'll miss out on so many opportunities to help others, just because the scope is small, or the impact is localized.

We shouldn't overlook the fact that there is a multiplier effect at work. Every small act, when combined with other actions, becomes more significant. After all, it takes one brick at a time to build anything—even something as monumental as the Great Wall of China or the Pyramids of Giza. All giant feats and major accomplishments are composed of numerous small steps. In the same way, charitable organizations recognize the importance of individuals. Although large grants often make up sizable portions of charities' budgets, small donors are very important. For one thing, attracting many small donors demonstrates broad support for a charity's work. In addition, over time, many small donations add up to a considerable sum. From a purely fundraising perspective, retaining 10,000 donors who give $100 each may actually be easier than courting— and keeping—a million-dollar contributor. Of course, in this book we do not look at legacy in financial terms, but rather in emotional ones of personal commitment and a sense of purpose.

In this chapter, we recognize and celebrate the "significance of small"—a phrase that I first heard from Patti Buss of One Hope, a small nonprofit founded by her husband, Steve, in Eugene, Oregon. A faith-based organization, One Hope engages local churches, businesses, and organizations to work together to positively affect the Eugene/Springfield area, which has a combined population of 375,000.

When asked what the significance of small means to her, Patti gave a thoughtful answer that frames this entire chapter discussion: "The significance of small for me is about never underestimating the small idea, the simple gesture," Patti said. "It would be really tragic if we think that only the big and grandiose are where we see the results. That's not true. The act of kindness, a word of encouragement—these are the small things that can also have a big impact."

Appreciation for the significance of small can empower you to start and build your legacy wherever you are, right now. It doesn't matter if you're in your 20s or 30s and trying to save for your first home while repaying your student loans—or if you are retired on a fixed income. Wealth is not a qualifier for building or sustaining a legacy. Anyone can give of themselves in many ways, such as volunteering in the community. The only prerequisite is caring about others.

It's true that any one individual, acting on their own, cannot save the world. However, when their efforts are combined with those of others, it makes a significant difference in the local community. And what is our world except a continuum of communities, encircling the globe?

WITHIN OUR "CIRCLE OF INFLUENCE"

Two of Stephen Covey's concepts from his book *The 7 Habits of Highly Effective People*[1]—"circle of concern" and "circle of influence"—apply to our discussion. The circle of concern is broad; it encompasses issues and problems that we care deeply about (for example, homelessness and poverty) or that affect us (such as climate change). But as ordinary individuals, we have little power to change what's within our circle of concern. As a result, it may be tempting to throw up our hands in frustration over not being able to do anything.

Our circle of influence, however, is much smaller and contains many things that we *can* control. When we shift from our circle of concern to our circle of influence, we stop being frustrated. We're no longer wasting our time and energy on what we cannot change and, instead, we're seeking to become more proactive where we can make a difference with positive results and better relationships.[2] We become more community-minded, seeing the problems and human needs where we live and work. This is where small really becomes significant.

ONE HOPE: MANY HANDS TO HELP OTHERS

One Hope, founded in 2008, takes a purposefully localized approach to serving the needs of its local community. Like many cities across America, Eugene, Oregon, and the surrounding area are a microcosm of national problems: poverty, homelessness, and food insecurity for low-income individuals and families. According to city statistics, more than 3,000 people in the Eugene area experience homelessness, and about 2,000 of them have no access to shelter at night. The causes are complex—"a lack of affordable housing, limited shelter capacity, and scarce mental and behavioral health resources . . ."[3] These are the "stubborn facts," as Patti called them, and "required a muscularity from a united church."

With the belief that it is possible to address even the most difficult problems in the community through a combination of prayer, reflection, discussion, and action, One Hope began its mission. It started by bringing together local churches of various denominations to determine how to respond to the community's needs. Over the years, One Hope's network of partners has expanded to include more churches, as well as nonreligious organizations and businesses. This is a twofold approach that increases awareness of local problems and rallies more support.

One Hope's outreach, known as Project Hope, focuses on low-income families in the Eugene-Springfield area. What began years ago as one church distributing donated shoes and school supplies to two local schools has expanded into an initiative that serves more than 3,000 students.

Imagine a school gymnasium, the floor lined with thousands of pairs of sneakers, sorted by size from the tiniest kindergarteners to the biggest high schoolers. The shoes are all new—donated or purchased with donations—and include top brands such as Vans, Adidas, and Nike. Add to that, new backpacks filled with school supplies, along with coats and jackets. When students come with their families to choose what they need for the school year, their excitement is palpable. For those students, including those in foster care or whose families struggle financially, hope looks like brand new sneakers and a backpack.

At Thanksgiving, One Hope deploys hundreds of volunteers to fill boxes with food and gift cards to purchase meat and perishables. In November 2023, One Hope gave away 1,300 boxes in the local community, although the need is much greater. "We could probably distribute 3,000 if we had a bigger space," Patti said.

More recently, One Hope has become a leading organization in a truly significant community project: Cottages of Hope to serve people as they transition out of homelessness. Built and installed by volunteers, Cottages of Hope are permanent structures at Everyone Village, an approximately four-acre parcel with the capacity of 75 individual tiny "cottages." As small as they are, measuring 16 feet by 8 feet, these dwellings are very significant to those who live in them and experience community, healing, and rehabilitation, while preparing to transition into "the next chapter in their story."[4]

The journey to create Cottages of Hope at Everyone Village is both intriguing and remarkable, grounded in a prior tragedy and the resilience of a community coming together. It began in 2020 with the catastrophic Holiday Farm fire that destroyed 173,000 acres and more than 500 homes and businesses.

Living Water Family Fellowship, a church near Blue River, Oregon, was among the countless buildings that burned to the ground. The only thing left standing on the church property was a storage shed—and out of the ashes of destruction, that sparked an idea: building sheds for people who had lost their homes. What followed was an outpouring of help from churches, businesses, contractors, building materials suppliers, and high school construction classes, along with nonprofits and other social organizations—for a total of 74 community partners.

Coordinating the effort, thanks to its extensive network of faith, business, and community leaders, was One Hope, working closely with three retired contractors who provided their expertise, mentorship, and leadership skills. They worked with anyone who wanted to help—such as a group of elementary school girls who wanted to build a shed or the businesspeople who came together anonymously to construct one of their own.

The project was called *Sheds of Hope,* with an initial goal of building 50 sheds. By June 2022, that goal was exceeded nearly threefold; 143 sheds funded, built, and installed by volunteers on the properties of those who had lost everything. The sheds were not meant to be dwellings, but rather a place for storing generators, tools, and anything salvaged from the site. "Those sheds were the first signs of hope on the properties where people had lost everything," said Steve Buss of One Hope. "It was a boost of encouragement."

When the project wrapped up, the question was what would be next. For months, One Hope's interfaith group had been praying for guidance on how to address the problem with homelessness in the Eugene area. "We prayed this prayer—that God would bring together government, church, nonprofit, and business to effectively shepherd unhoused people," Steve said.

The answer: Cottages of Hope at Everyone Village.

The catalyst for this project was Gabe Piechowicz, who has a pastoral background and was hired by the City of Eugene to address homelessness in the community through a network of government agencies, faith-based organizations, and private businesses. A local business donated a four-acre site, near where most of the homeless population congregated.

In the beginning, the site was used for unhoused people to park a camper or a car. As a long-term solution, however, that was insufficient as a step out of homelessness. That's when the connection was made to Sheds of Hope, and how that concept could be adapted to what became Cottages of Hope.

As Steve recalled, "We asked ourselves, what if we stretched that 8-by-8 shed to 8-by-16 and made it suitable for someone to live in?"

What ensued can only be described as a whirlwind of enthusiasm and commitment to turn the concept of a shed into a tiny cottage. Each has insulation, dry wall, electricity, a roof, two windows, and a door with a window—along with another key feature that helps create community: a tiny front porch. Basic furnishings include a bed and a dresser, along with a space heater and six outlets. Communal areas include showers and bathrooms, laundry facilities, and a kitchen.

Forty nonprofit groups provide wraparound services to villagers, including job training and placement, food programs, mental health support, and basic health programs. Most of the residents are single people, although a few couples do reside in the village. There are no families on site.

Volunteers construct a Cottage of Hope.
Source: Courtesy of One Hope.

Completed cottages, ready for occupancy.
Source: Courtesy of One Hope.

From an initial 27 cottages as of early 2024, the goal is to scale in the near term to 50 cottages, then eventually at least 75. "We want people to have dignity as they transition out of homelessness into living in a cottage," Steve said. "They can stay as long as they need—for years, if they need to." Some residents, however, have already successfully transitioned to jobs and low-income housing.

The community assembling around Everyone Village also encompasses a diverse group of donors and supporters, from church groups to local high schools, where students helping to build cottages are taught skills to become carpenters, electricians, and other trades.

This is the significance of small in action. In each effort, we find reminders of familiar metaphors that speak to the importance of even modest actions. There is the parable of the tiny mustard seed. Yet, even with faith that small, we're told, "You will say to this mountain, 'Move from here to there,' and it will move; and nothing will be impossible for you" (Matthew 17:20–21). Or the poor widow who offered "two mites"—a mite is estimated to be about 1/8 of a cent today—and yet her donation was far more generous than much larger amounts because it came out of her want, not her abundance (Mark 12:41–44). And, returning to the old fable of *Stone Soup* shared in the Introduction, we remember that when our offerings are combined with the gifts of others, the result is abundance.

The Big Impact of Small Things

The more we understand and appreciate the significance of small things, the more our perception changes. Our eyes and ears will be open to opportunities to help others. A neighbor or a colleague mentions a volunteer activity or a community drive, and the response is, "I'll help." We engage because we want to be part of the solution, instead of just talking about the problem.

That's what happened with Pat Commins, one of the people who assisted me in the research and writing of this book. Pat, who lives in Oregon, saw a post on Instagram from a group of local tattoo artists, who are friends of his. Pat frequently scrolls through their posts of artful designs, but one day something else caught his eye: the tattoo studio was collecting cold-weather supplies for people who are homeless.

This was Pat's call to action. He knew these artists and wanted to be supportive of what seemed like a worthy cause. However, Pat could not afford thousands of dollars in donations. And yet, Pat wanted to do whatever he could to help those who did not have a roof over their heads.

At the local Walmart, he bought a small tent, a couple of rain ponchos, and two sleeping bags. Then he added hand warmers and wool socks. The items filled the shopping cart as he wheeled toward the checkout. But while waiting in line, Pat saw how meager these supplies seemed compared to the enormity of homelessness in his community and across the country. Suddenly, his efforts felt futile.

There is no denying how entrenched social problems such as poverty and homelessness really are. According to a recent "point in time" report from the US Department of Housing and Urban Development, approximately 582,500 people experienced homelessness in the United States on a single night in 2022. Of that, about 60% were in emergency shelters, safe havens, or transitional housing. But 40% were "unsheltered"—meaning on the street, in abandoned buildings, or in what the report called "other places not suitable for human habitation."[5]

It seems inconceivable that, in one of the wealthiest countries, more than a half-million people are without a home or shelter. Against that sobering fact, Pat wondered what one shopping cart full of supplies would do?

Then something occurred to him. "It wasn't up to me—one person—to solve the larger issue. Rather, it was about doing what I could to help make our community a little bit better," he said.

When dropping off the supplies he'd just purchased for a total of $262, Pat noticed how few goods there were in the collection bin. After he unloaded his donations, though, that bin was filled with gear and clothing. "I knew what I'd given wouldn't last several years, let alone a lifetime, but it will help someone be warm and feel sheltered, even if it's only temporary," he said.

A few days after Pat dropped off supplies at the studio, he noticed another social media post that changed his perspective. The studio showed photos of collection bins from all around town brimming with cold weather gear and supplies. Here was tangible proof of the multiplier effect, an outpouring of care and concern.

Giving to Others

What we give to others is not limited to the tangible or the monetary. The gift of our time and talents can be priceless to the person who receives them. This enables anyone at any age, stage of life, or circumstance to give of themselves.

As I was working on this chapter in December 2023, my son, Daniel, came home for the holidays from the University of Notre Dame. Normally, Julie and I would have expected him to go off and see his friends who were also home from college. Instead, one of the first people Daniel went to see was Phil, a man in his late 80s who belongs to our parish church. They spent two hours at breakfast. When Daniel found out that Phil's wife was in the hospital, he went to visit her as well.

It's an unlikely connection. Phil is neither a neighbor nor a family member. Daniel didn't know him until a few years ago, during the COVID-19 pandemic. Concerned about older people in the parish, many of them in their 80s, Father Wayne Watts, our pastor, asked the seniors at the Catholic high schools to reach out to one or two people during the lockdowns. The phone calls were meant to be check-ins to say hello or to see if older people in the community needed any supplies, such as groceries. Daniel agreed to reach out to Phil, and soon they were having long conversations. They stayed in touch long after the lockdowns ended, and when Daniel went off to college, they continued to call each other regularly.

It's easy to imagine how much Phil enjoys having contact with a 21-year-old college student. Research studies and anecdotal evidence alike point to the importance of what's known as *intergenerational relationships*[6]—what I would have called "hanging out with my grandfather" when I was Daniel's age or even younger. Surprising for me was hearing Daniel's thoughts on what he receives in return. "I get a lot of wisdom and interesting stories from someone who grew up in a very different time and who is very supportive of me."

Daniel's comment is yet another reminder of legacy as a two-way street. Time and again, the people interviewed for this book spoke of being uplifted and transformed by those they served. In this way, what might be viewed as altruistic becomes holistic.

Sharing Our Gifts

As someone who has mentored many colleagues, students, and young professionals over the years, I can attest to how satisfying it is to help make a difference to someone along their life trajectory or when making key decisions. I always tell people (especially my students) that I don't claim to have the answers, only opinions. So, in "question-and-opinion" discussions, I do my best to listen and offer suggestions based on my own experiences and perspective.

PAYING IT FORWARD: BERKELEY COMMUNITY SCHOLARS

Mentoring is about being a sounding board—sometimes just listening to someone can help them clarify their thoughts and define their priorities. That's why mentoring is so impactful. As I tell my students, I was very fortunate to be mentored by people such as William Graham, chairman of Baxter International, and Donald Jacobs, the former dean of the Kellogg School of Management. If it weren't for these people who took the time and made the effort to guide me, I never would have had the opportunities that were offered to me. That's why I believe those of us who have been mentored have a moral responsibility to pay it forward by mentoring the next generation.

There are countless examples of mentoring programs—on college campuses, through alumni associations, in companies and professional organizations, and within communities. One, in particular, was brought to my attention by Stephen Isaacs, who is profiled in Chapter 6 and has a connection to the University of California at Berkeley and the Berkeley community. The program is called Berkeley Community Scholars. The name might give the impression that it's for students attending Berkeley. Rather, it's for young people who live in the *community* of Berkeley, California.

The organization started as the Berkeley Community Fund in 1991, with a mission to set up a fund for activist goals, such as social and economic justice, in the local community. In 2007, the fund changed its focus to helping graduates from Berkeley High School who were college-bound and faced challenges in seeing that possibility become a reality. Over the years, the organization recognized the importance of supporting students attending two-year community college and four-year institutions—both pathways to earning a bachelor's degree. In September 2019, the name was changed to Berkeley Community Scholars to reflect its mission.

The third executive director of Berkeley Community Scholars is Sherry Smith, an educational professional who has spent more than 40 years helping youth from underserved communities. Sherry's mission is to help students who live in the lowest economic households pursue and achieve their dreams of being accepted to, attending, and graduating from college. Her background includes working with students from the "most challenging" urban communities within California cities, including Los Angeles, Richmond, Oakland, and San Francisco. After joining Berkeley Community Scholars in 2019, her work continued to focus on creating pathways for "our most deserving, challenged, and under-resourced population of students."

Her work with Berkeley Scholars also reflects her family's legacy of service. "I come from a background of 'teachers and preachers'—from a place where you give because you are part of a community," Sherry said. "You don't judge the community—you don't know what people have had to overcome in their lives. You work to make that community as a whole better—and that means making sure the children are getting what they need to succeed."

Providing support for students while they are in college means so much more than just financial assistance. It also needs to include advising, mentoring, and access to social networks. Sherry gave the example of first-generation students (the first in their family to pursue a degree). "They are usually black and brown students who are underrepresented among college students in California and the US and come from families who are living in the lowest socioeconomic quartile," Sherry said.

Berkeley Community Scholars selects 30 to 40 students a year who are served by three full-time counselors. (Given that students may be anywhere from their first to their sixth year of college, this means on average a student population of about 125 served each year.) "We meet them where they are and walk beside them—not in front of or behind them," Sherry added.

The difference that the Berkeley Community Scholars makes in the life trajectory of the students can be seen in graduation rates. Among low-economic-status families and underrepresented student populations, the graduation rate in the United States is about 30% (compared to nearly 70% of their higher socioeconomic peers). However, Berkeley Community Scholars are graduating at a rate of 77%.

One of the supports Berkeley Community Scholars receive—and this is where volunteerism enters the picture—is each student is given a volunteer community mentor. What began as four or five volunteers who were friends of Berkeley Community Scholars board members has since grown to a diverse group of mentors, from retirees to recent graduates. The oldest mentors are in their 70s and the youngest is 26. They span all ethnicities, religions, and backgrounds. All are subject to thorough interviews and background checks.

"We recruit all year long—we never get all the mentors we need," Sherry said. "Our goal is to have every mentor work with the same student. We check with both the mentor and the mentees (the scholars) to ensure that the pairing is working for both parties."

Mentors are expected to have at least monthly contact with the students. This happens through a text, a phone call, a video chat, a walk, or over a cup of coffee or tea. These conversations are very helpful when students need advice, perspective, or encouragement. "It's a nice way to connect people of different generations—even if that's an 18-year-old with a 60-year-old," Sherry said. "With mentorship, there is an opportunity to see ourselves in someone else. With greater understanding and appreciation for others—especially those of different generations—we recognize the joy and tribulations of shared trajectories and journeys."

Peter Brock has been a mentor with Berkeley Community Scholars for 12 years, thanks to the encouragement and recommendation of an old friend, which resonated with his desire to pass on the guidance, support, and encouragement that have been so helpful to him and to his children.

"I'm excited to play a part in leveling the uneven opportunities in our society and enriching college campuses and the professional fields beyond with more diverse populations," Peter said. "By bolstering my mentees' confidence, perspective, and facility accessing available resources, I hope to elevate both their expectations of success and their ability to achieve it. I want to be part of a society where those with greater resources, experience and opportunity promptly reinvest those assets where they are in shorter supply, rewarding giver and receiver with lives freer of suffering, fuller of hope."

AN EXECUTIVE'S "OTHER JOB"

There are many ways to serve our local community, from food and clothing drives to cleaning up parks. There is also service that is far more significant. With no exaggeration, it can even be a matter of life and death. This was my thought when I spoke with Nick LoManto, one of my Kellogg students.

To put his story in perspective, we start with his "day job." For the past 13 years, Nick has worked for Vanguard, a global financial services firm, based in Malvern, Pennsylvania, 30 miles from Philadelphia. Vanguard is a household name among retail investors, with $7.7 trillion in assets under management. Founded by the late John Bogle, Vanguard has a reputation for putting its clients first, such as by developing no-cost and low-cost mutual funds. In his day job, Nick's title is head of High Net Worth Advice, leading a several-hundred person organization dedicated to helping clients reach their financial goals.

Then there is his "other job." He is a volunteer firefighter with the Ludwigs Corner Fire Company, serving three townships near Chester Springs, Pennsylvania. At the firehouse, he's not the guy in the button-down shirt. No one at the firehouse has any concept of him as an executive for a global financial institution.

"If you drew a Venn diagram—finance industry on one side and firefighter on the other—you'd see two different groups of people that don't overlap. Each is a different community," Nick explained.

At the firehouse, Nick is at the lowest level—a line firefighter. In fact, at age 36, Nick reported to a 23-year-old lieutenant of the fire company. "I mop floors, wash trucks, and take out the garbage at the firehouse," he said. And when a call comes in, Nick is on the firetruck with the rest of the crew, racing to the scene.

A minor incident such as a "culinary mishap" (another name for a small kitchen fire) may be extinguished within minutes. But when a major structure such as an apartment complex goes up in flames, Nick and his fellow firefighters could be on the scene for six or eight hours.

On average, being a volunteer firefighter is a commitment of 3 to 10 hours a week, including 2 to 3 hours for weekly training and drills, as well as being on standby at the firehouse. It's a significant time for this father of two young sons with a demanding job. There's no telling when he must race back to the firehouse in the middle of the night to get his gear and emergency equipment.

When I asked Nick how he came to be a volunteer firefighter, he explained the legacy he inherited from his service-oriented family. Both his grandfathers served in the military; one grandmother was a nurse, and the other adopted two children and supported veterans' organizations. His father retired from law enforcement, his mother teaches individuals who are blind or visually impaired, two sisters are nurses, and a third sister is a teacher.

"And there I was—a finance professional with every gift a person could wish for," Nick recalled.

The catalyst for deeper self-reflection in how he should serve was his father's retirement party in 2018, celebrating his career in law enforcement. Over the years, Nick's father had held several positions, including an emergency medical technician and working for a hospital system. "But Dad felt like there was a difference between his day job and what he was supposed to be doing," Nick explained.

His father found his calling. He took a huge pay cut (despite being the father of four) and became a special agent in counterterrorism work. "I knew a little bit about what he did, but Dad couldn't say much," Nick recalled.

For federal law enforcement officers, retirement is mandatory at age 57. It was at his father's retirement party that Nick learned more about the scope of his father's service when a coworker saluted him for working undercover to help put away "the bombmaker, bomb thrower, serial killer, crooked cop, and corrupt politician." That was the first concrete evidence of the significance of his father's service.

At the time, Nick was 29 years old, and he and his wife had just had their first child. On the three-and-a-half-hour drive home from the retirement party, Nick began asking himself deep questions: "What had I contributed? What example was I going to set for my children? What legacy would I leave?"

These questions drew Nick deeper into self-reflection as he began to see just how fortunate he and his wife really were. "We've been blessed with supportive families, working parents, close relationships with grandparents, healthy children, 'discounted' education [Nick and his wife were both student athletes with scholarships], and great careers."

At this point, Nick had done some volunteering; for example, he had coached youth sports. But he wanted to do more for his community. "That's when I had a conversation with a friend, who was a career firefighter. He asked me, 'Did you ever consider volunteer firefighting?' I was intrigued," Nick said.

It may come as a surprise to learn that most fire departments in the United States are staffed by volunteers. According to the National Fire Protection Association

(NFPA), a total of 1,041,200 firefighters were active in the United States in 2020. Of that total, 676,900 (65%) were volunteers, and only 364,300 (35%) were "career"—meaning firefighting is their profession.[7] The National Volunteer Fire Council highlights the importance of volunteer firefighters to their communities as "their first line of defense for many types of emergencies." These include fires, emergency medical calls, accidents, shootings, natural disasters, hazardous material incidents, water rescues, and other emergencies and service calls.[8]

In 2019, Nick visited the local firehouse for the first time. There he met mostly blue-collar men and women—some were farmers, others heavy-equipment operators. Instantly, Nick resonated with the team environment of "all showing up for each other," which he had experienced in sports. He had finally found his home for serving others.

Nick needed to complete 196 hours of in-person training to become certified as an interior firefighter (allowing him to enter the interior of a building, and not just fight fires from the outside). He also received training in first aid, CPR, hazardous materials, and vehicle rescues. "You respond to anything," Nick explained. "Fire is actually the least common. It could even be getting a cat off someone's roof."

When we spoke, Nick was five years into service and had spent many nights and weekends responding to accidents, rescues, emergencies, and fires. As grueling as the commitment might seem, Nick sees it as crucial for his life balance and keeping things in perspective. "This experience [as a firefighter] has made me a better leader and a better talent developer—including leading through chaos. Let's put it this way—when things 'blow up' in my day job, I can keep my head together because I've seen things really blow up as a firefighter."

His family remains very supportive of him, especially his wife, who understands that when a call comes, he must leave. His father relates to his firefighting, such as responding to emergency situations and dealing with life-and-death issues. His mother is also proud of him, but prefers not to think about the dangers he sometimes faces.

When Nick talked about his two sons—ages five and seven at the time of our interview—he once again began to reflect on his family's legacy of service. Although his sons are very young, Nick wonders where this legacy might take this next generation. "I'd love for them to grow up understanding this expectation," Nick said. "It doesn't matter what form it takes. Rather, it's what's expected in general. I hope they find a way to be of service."

For Nick, being a volunteer firefighter fulfills that need, despite being physically and intellectually demanding, and difficult emotionally. "But doing the hard things is worth it. It's what I want them to know. You have to do hard things— but make sure they're aligned with your values and skill set."

LOS ANGELES REGIONAL FOOD BANK: A SOLUTION WITHIN REACH

"This is a problem that everyone can do something about." These words from Michael Flood, who has served as the chief executive of the Los Angeles Regional Food Bank since 2000, are an invitation to self-reflection and to action. If we are motivated to make a difference, particularly within our local community, we are eager to learn more.

It starts with an understanding of food banks and how they work: collecting and distributing food for individuals, seniors, children, and families in need within a specific area—in Michael's case, Los Angeles County. Food banks uniquely bring together people in a community. The connection point is a basic human need: food. For Michael, this is a personal motivation as well.

"My parents emigrated to the US from Ireland. And if you know anything about Irish history—famines and the like—you can understand why providing food to others is important to me," Michael said.

He grew up in Los Angeles and attended the College of William & Mary in Virginia for his undergraduate degree in political science, and later returned for an MBA. After earning a business degree, though, he did not pursue the usual route. Instead, he was drawn to nonprofit work, first with a food bank in Northern California and then with the Los Angeles Regional Food Bank, which has been in operation for more than 50 years.

The Los Angeles Regional Food Bank traces its roots back to the late Tony Collier, a cook at a rehabilitation facility, who learned how to save money by soliciting food donations. Soon, he was inundated with food and started to give it to other charitable organizations. That surplus was the birth of the food bank.

It's a microcosm of an imbalance when it comes to food in the United States, where so much of the food that gets produced is not consumed. In fact, statistics show that food waste amounts to 80 million tons every year, equal to 149 billion meals. Said another way, that waste amounts to 38% of all the food produced and purchased in America.[9]

Food banks redistribute those resources by collecting from farmers, food companies, and retailers and distributing what would otherwise go to waste to those who struggle with food insecurity or poor nutrition. "Most food banks operate in a similar way: there's surplus food here and hungry people there. You have to find a way to put them together," Michael said.

As of 2024, there are more than 400 food banks that provide food and services to 63,000 pantries and shelters across the United States. That number is huge compared to 40 years ago when there were only two dozen food banks in the entire country. Despite this large increase in food aid, however, the level of food insecurity has remained consistent for the last 30 years. This is why food banks remain a crucial part of the solution to hunger in local communities.[10]

Like most nonprofits, food banks are part of a bigger network across a community. About half the organizations the Los Angeles Regional Food Bank works with are faith-based and the other half are community groups. It also works closely with schools and health clinics, as well as with local government to help provide assistance to people in need.

Food banks differ in scale from a food pantry, which typically occupies a storage room or even a closet at a community organization or place of worship, where people can seek assistance directly. But the intention is the same: providing food to address immediate hunger or until the next paycheck, Social Security check, or government assistance arrives.

To give a visual, Michael compared the food bank as "walking into a Costco" and seeing coolers and freezers and long shelves of shelf-stable products. But instead of shoppers wheeling carts around the aisles, a food bank has dozens of volunteers who are crucial to getting supplies into the community. Often, this means shipping to partner agencies who make direct distributions to individuals and families.

By the nature of what they do, food banks have a relatively small circle of influence. Their significance comes from the impact they have on people who may be wondering where their next meal is coming from. For the Los Angeles Regional Food Bank, that significance is further amplified by its longevity. Over the 50 years of its existence, the Los Angeles Regional Food Bank has collected and distributed more than 2 billion pounds of food, which is equivalent to about 1.6 billion meals. These numbers are significant—and so is the ongoing need.

An Evolving Program

Prior to the pandemic, demand for food went up and down with the economy; the strength or weakness of the economy was an indicator of demand for food assistance. The pandemic, however, suddenly made food insecurity an issue for more people, including those who had never experienced it before. Add to that inflation and an escalating cost of living—especially in places like California—and it's no wonder that more individuals, senior citizens, and families now require food assistance.

To illustrate, the University of Southern California has undertaken a study of food insecurity in Los Angeles County. In the heart of the pandemic, from April to December 2020, some 40% of low-income households in the area were food insecure, a large increase from 27% for all of 2018. In 2021, food insecurity declined slightly, then rose again to 24% in 2022 and 30% as of the first half of 2023. This translates to more than 1 million households and 44% of low-income individuals in Los Angeles County being considered food insecure. In other words, for them, putting food on the table is a daily struggle.[11]

The traditional staples of food banks are canned goods and other shelf-stable products. But increasingly, food banks are moving more heavily into fresh produce, which is highly nutritious and expensive to buy.

Moving from ensuring people are consuming enough calories to providing better nutrition is especially helpful for those who live in what are called *food deserts*. These are areas—from inner cities to remote rural areas—where there is not sufficient access to affordable, nutritious food. A family living in an underserved area may have only a convenience store within walking distance. Distribution of healthier foods within that community improves access and represents an evolution in the mission and operation of food banks. Increasingly, there is an intentional focus on fresh produce to improve nutrition and help prevent chronic health conditions such as diabetes and hypertension.

Providing more fresh food has also meant expanding relationships with farmers, growers, and grocery stores. "Everybody in the food business gets it—they hate to see food go to waste," Michael said. "For growers and farmers, it's their sweat and hard work that goes into fresh food. The response to donating surplus is very positive."

A Legacy Beyond Self

Although Michael is the public face of the organization, he is quick to say rather emphatically, "It's not about me." He gives all the credit to the staff and some 20,000 volunteers, many of whom have been helping for several years—and some for two decades or more. "We're an organization that does good things. The work we do is about purpose, having an impact and helping others. That's what makes it enjoyable," he added.

From donating to a food drive to pitching in at a food pantry or food bank, anyone can find a way to help in their community. In fact, food banks and food pantries may be among the easiest and most accessible ways to get involved.

"It's serving person to person, family to family," Michael said. "Over time, the numbers get big. But in the end, it's still individuals. On one side, it's the volunteers who are committed to help. And on the other side, it's the people who are getting that assistance." For an individual who has to choose between buying food or paying rent, for the family struggling to feed their children, this help is tangible—and very, very significant.

WHAT NEED DO YOU SEE?

If we look around the world, there are so many problems—most of them global in scale and scope. It's easy to become discouraged, thinking there is nothing we can do to help. But when we shift our focus from global to local, we see those macro problems on a micro scale.

If we're concerned about hunger and poverty, we are drawn to the local food bank or other community organization. If we're concerned about gaps in educational achievement, we think about the opportunity to tutor or mentor others. If we worry about security and safety, we think about joining a volunteer organization, such as the local fire company.

It all comes down to our personal passions that meet the pain in the community. To experience the significance of small, we only need to reflect on what we are most passionate about.

- *Within our community, what concerns, challenges, and needs resonate with us?*

- *What organizations are looking for help?*
- *What volunteer activities do our friends engage in that we might want to learn more about or try?*

And remember, even if those efforts seem small or localized, they are still significant.

CHAPTER 4

GROWING AT
THE GRASSROOTS

Fog crept along the dirt road to the site where, on an October morning, 12 volunteers gathered to help restore a wetland habitat. What was once a family farm was purchased by the McKenzie River Trust, an organization whose name reflects its mission: entrusted with the health and sustainability of the land surrounding the McKenzie River, a 90-mile-long waterway in western Oregon.

On Wednesday mornings, from early fall through late spring, a group of dedicated volunteers works at the site known as Green Island, which sits where the McKenzie and Willamette Rivers intersect in the Willamette Valley. This was no coffee-and-donuts gathering. The only things passed out to volunteers, ranging in age from early 30s to mid-80s, were heavy gloves, shovels, saws, and long-handled clippers. Then, for two-and-a-half hours, they trimmed branches and eradicated blackberry vines that seemed to consume every other shrub and tree.

McKenzie River Trust volunteers work on the watershed.
Source: Courtesy of McKenzie River Trust; photo credit Steve Smith
Photography.

The fieldwork that day was part of the McKenzie River
Trust's long-term plans for the Green Island property. Spring
runoff and heavy rains that caused frequent flooding and
turned the property to mud made it unsuitable for farming—
but perfect as a watershed habitat. The trust bought the
property in 2003 and then added more acreage, for a total of
1,100 acres at the site. Since 2006, the trust has converted
more than 850 acres of Green Island from agricultural fields
to forested floodplain. Thus far, more than 1 million native
trees and shrubs have been planted, and more will grow
there as part of the trust's vision to restore and protect the
watershed habitat for otters, beavers, deer, and other animals, along with fish, reptiles, and amphibians. The healthier the land and the creatures it supports, the healthier
the river.

This is what it means to establish and sustain a legacy at the grassroots. In this chapter, we will visit three such endeavors that focus on sustainability in the most basic of human needs—water and food. First, we will spend some time with the McKenzie River Trust and its work helping protect the sole source of drinking water for more than 200,000 people in and around the City of Eugene, home of the University of Oregon. Among its other projects the trust also works in several watersheds across western Oregon, including much of the central coast.

Then we move on to India and an organization known as Kheyti (which means farming in Hindi) that is helping smallholder farmers raise more crops, despite drought and extreme temperatures due to climate change. (Smallholder farmers are those who raise crops or animals on very small plots of land, often only a few acres.) After that, our attention turns to Malawi, in East Africa, where a small quail farm provides protein for a rural community. The three projects—in Oregon, India, and Malawi—show how the grassroots grow. Problems confronting local people are addressed with possible solutions. Success is never guaranteed; often, there is a great deal of trial and error. But with persistence, lessons learned, and the support and passion of donors and volunteers, an idea takes root and grows into a sustainable project.

Working on the local level, these projects address urgent needs for today while also establishing a legacy of better sustainability for tomorrow. Through conversations with organizers, volunteers, and supporters, it also became clear that these endeavors satisfy another basic human need—community. Food and water are not the only essentials to our survival; so is human connection, such as soothing words, a warm embrace, and eye contact. In fact, we cannot survive without these critical elements of forming attachment.

McKENZIE RIVER TRUST: PROTECTING THE LAND AND WATER

The source of the McKenzie River is runoff from melting snow and glaciers in the Cascade Mountains of eastern Oregon. From there, its pure water flows through scenic, rugged beauty that attracts fishermen and whitewater enthusiasts. But the McKenzie also means life to both wild creatures and communities. In this time of climate change, when lower rainfalls and urban development present urgent challenges to rivers used as water sources, protecting the McKenzie has become a high priority.

The McKenzie River Trust was founded in the late 1980s when a local landowner and an environmental leader brought together a group of concerned citizens who shared the mission of preserving the river for generations to come. The trust's landholdings grew from an initial 11 acres to nearly 10,000 acres as of 2024 across western Oregon, including the Willamette Valley, central coast, and Umpqua watershed.

The Land Trust Alliance counts as its members 948 land trusts in the United States, of which the McKenzie River Trust is one. Combined, these community-led trusts have conserved a total of about 60 million acres over the pasts four years—larger than all the land contained in US national parks. The Land Trust Alliance has set a goal of conserving another 60 million acres by the end of the 2020s.[1]

"The land is where it all starts," said Elizabeth Goward, who is the community engagement manager for the McKenzie

River Trust. "It's not just for wealth-building. Every part of our lives is dependent on land."

Trusts hold their land in perpetuity. This refers not only to ownership that conceivably lasts forever but also speaks to the mission of conserving natural resources for countless future generations. But simply holding the land does not suffice. "When you talk about perpetuity, we can't have that if nobody cares," Elizabeth said. "If nobody has that feeling—that the land is special and dear to you—you can't really say that it's being protected in perpetuity. That's why we invest in community engagement programs, including our volunteer programs."

It takes people who are willing to get involved, especially dedicated volunteers who work on the land. "There are all kinds of folks—PhDs in chemical science to cabinetmakers," explained Elizabeth. "They all want to be part of something they care about and choose to volunteer."

Thinking Globally, Acting Locally

On a particular "Watershed Wednesday" at Green Island, after brief introductions and a discussion of the morning's work, volunteers moved into a grove of cottonwoods and maple trees to cut deadwood and yank out what seemed like miles of blackberry vines. This was roll-up-your-sleeves volunteerism for people who probably could have put their time and effort into any number of activities, including those that would result in less mud and fewer sore muscles.

About half the volunteers that day were retirees who seek both community and a way to give back; many of them have been volunteering for the trust for years. One was Dan Robinhold, a retired cardiologist, who said he has always preferred volunteer activities that were water-related and involved outdoor work. Now in his mid-80s, Dan volunteers two or three half-days per week, including with the McKenzie River Trust.

Sheila and Kane, both in their 30s, were among the newer volunteers. "I've lived in Oregon for four years and have been looking for the right organization, one that values beauty and recreation," Sheila explained. "I also want to move my body and be active while doing something good."

Kane added, "I moved to this area for the recreational beauty. Having a background in environmental science, I knew I wanted to give back to the outdoor community. But I've been so busy working on building businesses that I haven't really had time to give back."

There they were, hacking away at thick blackberry vines that had completely overtaken a 10-foot cottonwood. The tree and this vine had been fiercely competing, and the tree was losing the battle. Tangled vines and sharp thorns slowly lifted away as volunteers cut deeper into the blackberry thicket and the tree emerged. More than an hour later, the sweaty work of four people had managed to free one tree—with many more to go. But with each small improvement, the trees can thrive, protecting soil, water, and wildlife—the entire ecosystem of the river.

The volunteers at Green Island demonstrated what an individual can do in their own backyard, where the impact can be seen and felt. It is the epitome of thinking globally and acting locally. The efforts these volunteers put forth week after week accumulate over time into a legacy for generations to come.

While climate change and other ecological problems continue to affect our planet, it's easy to become overwhelmed—to wring our hands and wait for someone to do something. At the grassroots, though, everyone has a part to play. "When we talk about climate change, it's so big. It's hard to know where and how you can make an impact," Elizabeth said. "But through the watershed, people can get involved with other passionate people."

In addition to the hands-on work by volunteers, the McKenzie River Trust offers hikes on some of its land and limited-mobility tours for those who cannot hike. "We are invested in all the ways that people can connect with the land," Elizabeth added. "People and land have always been together. We're all part of the landscape. Every decision we make—the food we eat, what we're wearing—everything can be traced back to the land you're on."

To be a steward is also to confront the uncomfortable aspects of American history, of lands taken from Indigenous people by white settlers. As the trust states on its website, "It's important to acknowledge our past so that we may work towards a more just and equitable future." Today, the trust is working with local Tribes on land protection to provide access to land for cultural purposes and to restore some properties to Tribal ownership. As conversations occur and relationships build, people have been able to learn about Indigenous knowledge and practices for caretaking land and water.

The Living River

To capture the purpose and essence of this work, Elizabeth referred to a concept called *the living river*. As she explained, over decades and even centuries, humans have changed rivers, redirecting their natural flow into channels made deeper and wider for navigation and shipping freight by boat and barge. Now, restoration seeks to reverse that so-called improvement, allowing rivers to flow more freely and nature to restore its balance. "Every single change the river makes supports something new," Elizabeth said. "As a new side channel in the river is formed, that's a changing habitat. An oxbow forms, and it becomes home to turtles and dragonflies."

There is humility in stewardship. Humans are far from infallible, so some mistakes are inevitable. The most we can expect of ourselves is to do the right thing, and to do so the best way we can. Elizabeth gave the example of how removing wood, such as felled trees, from rivers and streams was once viewed as the right thing to do. Now, however, that wood is being put back in to help salmon, such as the spring chinook in the McKenzie River, access habitat for laying their eggs. Successful rearing habitat requires protected places in the river where the current is not so swift, and food can be captured and held within the system. This also supports young salmon to grow strong for their journey to the ocean.

As new practices are adopted, nature is often the best teacher for those who are willing to be still and observe. "If I want to talk about wetland restoration, I talk about the beavers. Not only are they cute and charismatic, but what we are doing in our work on the river is what the beavers do—we just work on a bigger scale," Elizabeth said. "We watch beavers coming out of their lodges and how they impact the ecosystem by building dams, and we can replicate this work to help speed the recovery of natural systems."

The trust has done much the same thing as the beavers at a site known as Finn Rock Reach. What looks like a messy cluster of logjams is actually an ideal habitat of slow-moving water where fish can hatch and mature.

Elizabeth drew a parallel between restoring the natural flow of a river and what it means to live a good life—one that is dynamic and can shift course. Just like a living river is allowed to change course and flow into the wetlands, so too we can reclaim our own freedom to grow and explore, as we allow the current of life to change us. Often, this is how we find true purpose in our lives.

KHEYTI: BRINGING CLIMATE RESILIENCE TO SMALL FARMERS IN INDIA

Saumya was working as an investment banker in India when an abrupt realization occurred to her. "I didn't want to do this for the rest of my life." For some time, she had been pondering the nagging question of where to find more purpose, and with some self-reflection a new direction began to unfold.

While at the investment bank, Saumya became involved in its corporate social responsibility unit, with weekend projects such as working with underprivileged children and becoming more aware of the victims of human trafficking. "That work made me feel so happy," Saumya recalled. "My weekends were my redemption."

Wanting that sense of fulfillment in more areas of her life, Saumya quit her job and began exploring where and how she could make a difference. She had grown up in Bihar, one of the poorest states in India, where her father had worked in government service. Following his advice, Saumya began volunteering with a microfinance project. That led her to join a social enterprise in New Delhi, working with rural youth, many of whom were children of farmers, who could not complete their schooling.

The social enterprise had the idea of putting these young people through three-month vocational courses—such as in plumbing and welding—with the goal of helping them find employment. That uncovered another problem: after receiving training, young people left rural areas to find jobs in cities but usually didn't make enough money to live in urban areas and had to return to their villages.

At the same time, millions of people have been leaving India to work as manual laborers in the Middle East or Singapore, often living in substandard conditions and losing a portion of their salaries to a middleperson who facilitated the migration. This gave Saumya an idea: training workers in India and contracting with large companies abroad to employ them. The result was a pilot program to train welders and electricians for a shipyard. But the project never expanded beyond the pilot. "The system was too set in its ways," Saumya said.

After suffering what she called her "first failure" in social enterprise, Saumya began applying to business schools and enrolled in Northwestern University's Kellogg School of Management in 2015. Just prior to beginning her studies, Saumya and some friends had been working on a startup idea they called Kheyti. Saumya spent her breaks from Kellogg in India to work on the fledgling project and then, after graduating in 2017, went back to India full time and fully devoted to Kheyti.

It's important to understand that, given her previous experience in investment banking and an MBA from Kellogg, Saumya could have pursued any number of jobs in finance, consulting, or other fields and earned a much higher salary. But her commitment to making a change in the lives of smallholder farmers in India was unshakeable.

As one of four partners in Kheyti, Saumya talked to farmers about their issues and challenges. "We spoke to a thousand farmers around the country. Whenever we asked, 'What are your challenges?' their response was some form of climate change, although they didn't use those words. They said things like, 'We could predict the monsoons before' and 'The summers are hotter now.'"

No matter how much hard work these farmers put in, their crops often didn't produce enough and sometimes failed completely. In response, Kheyti's mission evolved: how to make farming more predictable and sustainable—both environmentally and for the farmers needing to feed and support their families.

Adding to the challenges were the traditional practices in India, whereby land is passed down from a father to his sons. Over time, landholdings get subdivided into smaller and smaller parcels. Today, the average holding is about five acres, but some of the farmers Kheyti works with have even less acreage.

Kheyti needed to deliver an affordable solution to help farmers make the most of small plots of land and to do so at a time of climate extremes. Kheyti chose greenhouses because there was ample proof of concept, such as in the Western Hemisphere where greenhouses are used to start seeds and grow plants during cold weather and extreme winters. In India, this concept could be adapted to help farmers grow crops in extreme heat, with less water. Because plants grow vertically in greenhouses, that means less bending and physical labor, particularly for women who do much of the actual farming. "And since the greenhouse sits on the land by their homes, women can spend a few hours a day in the greenhouse and be at home, taking care of their families, the rest of the time," Saumya said.

Making an Affordable Solution

The concept was clear: greenhouses would be a workable solution for smallholder farmers, except for one significant barrier: the cost. "Greenhouses were only accessible to big farmers and rich farmers," Saumya explained. "Our goal was to make greenhouses affordable and accessible to small farmers." When Kheyti approached greenhouse companies about making a smaller, more affordable structure, the cost was still too high at $3,000. Then Kheyti approached several banks about making loans for the purchase of the greenhouses, and the answer was usually no because smallholder farmers do not have a credit history. The only way the banks would make the loans was if Kheyti underwrote the entire loan value and recovered the loans from farmers, which was beyond what the organization could do.

Then COVID struck, and all lending froze in India, especially financing to smaller farmers. At this juncture, and amid a global health crisis that was particularly severe in populous places such as India, Kheyti could have moved on to some other project—or, perhaps, given up altogether. What happened next demonstrates the power of the grassroots, infused with the desire to help local people help themselves.

Kheyti used the COVID shutdown to rethink the entire greenhouse concept. It brought together a team of designers, some of them in Israel and the Netherlands, and came up with something that could deliver 70% of the efficiency of the $3,000 model, but cost only $650, or less than 100,000 rupees. With help from donors to subsidize the greenhouse purchases, more smallholder farmers could afford what Kheyti believed to be a workable solution.

"We built this greenhouse for the crops that the farmers were growing—like onions, potatoes, and cauliflower—versus specialty crops that are usually grown in [larger, commercial] greenhouses like peppers, zucchini, and flowers," Saumya explained.

Farmers also provided their input on the design of the greenhouse, telling Kheyti what they did and did not need to grow basic crops. Eliminating unnecessary features simplified the design and reduced the cost. "We pride ourselves on being close to our customers," Saumya said. "It's basically involving them whenever we are doing anything."

What makes Kheyti so admirable is how it empowers farmers at the grassroots. As we'll see with One Acre Fund (in Chapter 7), which is helping farmers in Africa improve their yields and feed their families, the secret to success is engaging with those who are closest to the problem to discern the right solution. "I feel that is the way to build any product or solution—listen to the ideas of farmers," Saumya said.

Through 2021, Kheyti worked with 500 farmers in one state in India. After launching their low-cost product in 2022, they were able to add 1,300 farmers. As of this writing, Kheyti had 3,000 greenhouses across 11 states in India, helping farmers grow as much as seven times more food, while using 90% less water. "At the end of five years, we want to reach 100,000 farmers," Saumya said.

Achieving that goal will require Kheyti to engage others in this grassroots endeavor. By raising money from donors, Kheyti aims to provide $300 in subsidies to reduce the net cost of each greenhouse to $350. "This will put more greenhouses on the land of more farmers, including those with the smallest plots of land," Saumya said.

And, as the greenhouse project rolls out, Kheyti aims to show the Indian government what is possible for creating a larger scale, with hopes of one day garnering government subsidies as well.

From the Grassroots to Global Recognition

As a nonprofit organization, Kheyti is supported by a donor base that includes several foundations. Thanks to this network, one of Kheyti's donors nominated the organization for The Earthshot Prize, a prestigious environmental award that is sponsored by Prince William of the United Kingdom. In 2022, after a 10-month selection process and more than 1,000 nominations reviewed by an expert panel of advisors, Kheyti was chosen as the winner of Earthshot's "Protect and Restore Nature" category. It received £1,000,000, as well as a pledge of support from the Earthshot Prize Global Alliance, a network of leading global philanthropies, nongovernmental organizations, and private sector businesses.

"I feel we were really lucky," Saumya said. "Even though we don't have a huge scale—we only have a few thousand farmers—we were selected for this prestigious prize."

After spending time talking with Saumya, it became clear that luck had very little to do with receiving this recognition. What made all the difference was Kheyti's determination to empower and equip smallholder farmers, enabling them to grow their crops despite mounting environmental challenges.

"If you look at agriculture, the solutions being offered today such as apps for farmers only touch about the top 10% of farmers. We're working with the smallest land holders," Saumya said. "It's hard, but I don't see any other way."

By working with farmers who are trying to eke out a living on only a few acres, Kheyti epitomizes how to establish a legacy at the grassroots. "If I can help one family send their kids to school or put a proper roof over their heads, that's what keeps us going," Saumya said. "And when farmers can stay in their villages and grow enough to feed their families and make a living—that is a legacy that they can give to their children."

MALAWI: A "BIG" IDEA AT THE GRASSROOTS

The photo shows a yellow quail chick with streaks of darker feathers cradled in a hand. Its body is so tiny, the bird barely covers half the person's palm. But this small bird is part of a lifeline for an entire village in Malawi in East Africa, and all because of an idea that emerged at the grassroots.

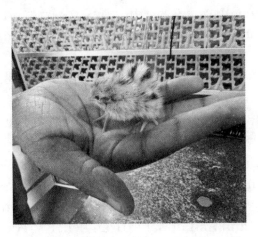

Quail chick at Umodzi Poultry.
Source: Courtesy of Umodzi Poultry and Steve Isaacs.

"There was a lady who told me about this little bird called a quail. She praised it so much. But they couldn't raise it [in her rural village] because quail do not sit on their own eggs. So to raise quail, they needed incubators and electricity," explained Mathews Tisatayane, who grew up in Malawi, and then came to the United States with his American wife. Today he helps run Umodzi Poultry, a bird hatchery in rural Malawi that began operations in June 2022.

A few years ago, however, it was only an idea—a kind of intriguing puzzle that needed a solution. As it turned out, Mathews had the life experience, knowledge, connections, and passion to pursue what he called *BIG*—birds, insects, and gardening—to support a village in Malawi.

When asked how it all began, Mathews went back to the beginning of his own story. He described the life experiences and early influences that directly affected his perspective on helping others and his career choices. In listening to his story, we can hear the same kind of calling that so often happens at the grassroots: confronting an urgent problem with innovation and initiative to find a solution.

Mathews's personal story began in rural Malawi. As a young boy, he looked up to his great uncle, who had been a successful farmer and helped provide for more than 1,000 tenants on his land. Mathews recalled children in that village who had emigrated from neighboring countries, including those escaping war in Mozambique. This exposed him to many different languages and religions—Hinduism, Islam, Christianity, and traditional African beliefs. "These were not divisions, but brought the people together around the celebrations," Mathews recalled. "People were very open-minded and welcoming of those who were different."

From a young age, Mathews liked learning, even sneaking off at age seven to the local school, five miles away. "My mom said, 'you're too young,' so I started on my own," he recalled with a laugh. When the headmaster questioned him, because he had not enrolled and paid tuition, Mathews explained how much he wanted to be in school. "I see you like school—you will go far," the headmaster told him. "I will allow you to attend."

During Mathews's third year of high school in 1993, however, his great uncle died. Suddenly, this man who had supported the entire family and so many others was gone. Mathews lost his source of tuition, with only one year left to finish high school. Instead of becoming discouraged, Mathews started on his first entrepreneurial venture. He approached a farmer with a pig and offered to slaughter it and bring the meat to market for a share of the money. They agreed, and Mathews did exactly what he'd promised, and soon others in the village asked him to butcher and sell their animals. He built trust and earned enough money to finish high school.

Mathew's grades were good enough to go to college, but with a change in the Malawian government and its policies, going to university was beyond his reach. Instead, he received training as a teacher and taught for seven years. Then, through a friend, he was introduced to an American woman, who had come to Malawi as a Peace Corps volunteer. After they married, Mathews and his wife moved to the United States.

Inspired by his wife's example, Mathews sought out volunteering opportunities in the San Francisco area, where they lived. He began working with HIV/AIDS patients in a hospital. "Doing that, I saw the passion of the nurses. And I saw people at the end of their lives—some of them had nothing. But there was a nurse sitting next to them, saying, 'I am here, listening to you.'"

Mathews found the direction he had been seeking and began taking prerequisites for nursing school. After graduating from the University of San Francisco with a bachelor of science in nursing, Mathews spent 10 years with the San Francisco Department of Public Health. But he felt a pull to do even more.

Although Mathews had been in the United States for 19 years, he traveled frequently to Malawi. On one such visit, he accompanied a friend who was investigating using solar power to provide lighting in rural areas in Malawi. The solar project never got off the ground. But the $2,000 that Mathews and his friend had committed to that project ended up channeled to a different cause. Mathews's sister helped them provide that money to women who were in need of funds. "We did not even ask what the money was going to be used for. We didn't even want any thanks," Mathews said.

Two years later, when Mathews returned to Malawi, he was greeted by his sister and nine other women, all dressed alike. These local women had used the $2,000 to start a microfinancing project. The projects they financed ranged from raising poultry to serving tea. It was from one of these women that Mathews first heard about raising quail. "It takes only two months from egg to table. That makes it a very good food source for the poor," he said.

While still working as a nurse in San Francisco at the time, Mathews returned to the United States with an idea of providing solar power to generate electricity for the incubators. The initial test, however, was not successful. The solar equipment didn't have adequate battery storage to power the incubators at night. "That is the failure I suffered. It was one of the most painful things," Mathews recalled. "But I had gained the trust in the women. And I knew we were going in the right direction."

When the pandemic hit the United States, as a public health nurse Mathews provided care to homeless people who tested positive for COVID and needed temporary housing as they recuperated. "During this time, I had this realization. What if this [disease] becomes the end of me? Have I realized the maximum of my potential? Is this the best way to help the poor?" Mathews recalled.

This is the kind of existential question that leads to self-reflection. Often, we are so busy and moving so fast, it is easy to get overwhelmed. It is times like this, as mentioned in Chapter 2, we need to slow down to make sure that we distinguish between activity and productivity. It becomes an invitation to reflect on what matters most and the difference we want to make to others, our community, and even the world.

Mathews reached out to Daniel Kammen, an expert in renewable energy, who serves as the Distinguished Professor of Energy at UC Berkeley. Also at this time, Mathews learned about a new master's degree program in development engineering. "I said bingo! I will try. I'm not an engineer, but a nurse. But I like solving complex problems." After his acceptance into the program, Mathews needed financial help; among those who reached out was Stephen Isaacs, an American entrepreneur and philanthropist who supports many projects in Africa (and whose story is shared in Chapter 6).

The more Mathews and Steve talked, the more common ground they discovered: the role of women in society, food security, wealth disparities across countries and among individuals. "We just started talking about all of this," Mathews recalled. "It's like walking to your destination and you don't know who is walking with you. But this person fits into your life like a brother. Stephen has been behind me: paying for my education, investing in my country, and coming to my country."

When Mathew tried to thank Steve for all he had done, he received quite an unexpected response. "He told me, 'Mathews, the benefit is symbiotic. I get more help than I give. There is no giving without receiving, and no receiving without giving.'"

In 2023, Mathews left his nursing job to concentrate full time on Umodzi Poultry. The key to its success was solving the solar power issue, generating about 25 kilowatts, which is sufficient not only for the hatchery but also for a pump to provide water for irrigation and drinking—the latter being a resource for everyone in the village.

As the hatchery raised quail successfully, Mathews and his team found more ways to promote sustainability through his BIG model. The *B* stands for birds, specifically quail, chickens, and a new experiment, ducks. The *I* is for insects, raised for poultry feed and pollination. The *G* refers to gardening, growing legumes, peanuts, sweet potatoes, and grains (droppings from the bird coops are a natural fertilizer source).

The community impact goes beyond an important food source; Umodzi also provides regular jobs to 25 to 30 workers, as well as casual labor on a day-to-day basis. "We hire local people. We are the only ones that can provide that service within five square miles where there are no jobs."

Although the budget is small, the money is spread as far as possible. Ten percent of Umodzi's total sales is pledged to the women's microfinance project (now government certified) to create even greater impact. "My goal is to expand through these women so they can help another person, and then another group and another group," Mathews said. "The solar electricity is deployable anywhere. All I would ask is that we don't do anything without the cooperation of the women."

It's a lesson Mathews has learned firsthand: empowering women equates to economic empowerment of a community and sustainability at the grassroots. To explain, Mathews posed a rhetorical question: "Do you want the money I give you, or the money you work for?" The answer in his mind is obvious. "We want to work for our money. You have dignity— it gives you humanity. The money that is just given to you does not satisfy you as a human being."

AS THE GRASSROOTS GROWS . . .

The problems and issues confronting our world often appear so large as to be almost insurmountable. It can seem impossible for any individual to make a difference. And yet, in these three stories, we see examples of people who, rather than becoming overwhelmed or waiting for large institutions to intervene, decided that they could make a difference, starting in their own backyard.

This brings us back to the McKenzie River Trust and its Watershed Wednesday project. The fieldwork in this riparian habitat is a reminder that a legacy is not for humans alone but also for every other creature that inhabits this land, often without a person in sight. This kind of legacy teaches us to give back to our nonhuman neighbors on this planet, and to make sure there is a future for all who will inherit the Earth.

That kind of stewardship may sound like a grand plan, but it was visible among the dozen volunteers who toiled long and hard to free one tree at a time from the overgrowth of blackberry vines. One of the volunteers was Anita Larson, a retired teacher. She has engaged in many volunteer activities over the years but explained that she gravitated toward the McKenzie River Trust because "I agree with the mission."

As the work session for that day wound down, Anita kept cutting away at one more blackberry vine, and then another and another. Finally, the tree was free. "Well, at least we helped that one," Anita said, smiling.

Her comment recalled a well-known fable I heard many years ago. As the story goes, a young man walked along a beach where the receding tide had left thousands of starfish stranded on the sand.[2] One by one, the young man reached down, picked up a starfish, and tossed it back into the ocean. An older person on the same beach saw the young man and asked what he was doing. The young man explained that the sun was up, and the tide was going out; if he didn't get the starfish back into the water, they would die.

The beach was miles long, the older person said, and there were countless starfish along it. He couldn't possibly expect to make a difference, let alone save them all. Undeterred, the young man reached for a starfish and threw it into the ocean. "I made a difference to that one."

No matter how small the immediate impact, it should not be underestimated. Over time, every grassroots endeavor not only supports the local community, but also becomes part of a much larger whole that can help change the world.

And so we ask ourselves:

- *What are the issues that are close to our hearts and weigh on our minds?*
- *Where are the grassroots connections to addressing those issues?*
- *Whom do we know who can make a connection or introduction to help us learn more and get involved?*

CHAPTER 5

FROM LOSS
TO LEGACY

There is a time for everything, and a season for every activity under the heavens: a time to be born and a time to die, a time to plant and a time to uproot . . .

—Ecclesiastes

It is a picture worth far more than 1,000 words—this one speaks volumes. In the photograph, a handsome young man and his mother smile into the camera. Their connection is instantly visible in their similar facial features, as well as the way they sit so relaxed together. Looking at this photo, we can easily imagine this picture being taken on a family vacation.

The deeper meaning can only be grasped in the context of where this photo is displayed: on the website of the Christopher Wolf Crusade, named for the smiling young man in the photograph. Tragically, in 2016, Christopher Wolf died at the age of 32 from an accidental opioid drug overdose. For 14 years prior to his death, Christopher struggled with an addiction that started with a pain medication prescribed to

Christopher Wolf and Cammie Wolf Rice.
Source: Courtesy of Cammie Wolf Rice.

him in a hospital following surgery for ulcerative colitis. Years of battling that addiction, including the best rehabilitation his family could obtain for him, did not stop the unthinkable from occurring. His life ended far too soon.

When we know the backstory of the photo, our perspective changes. Now we see it as yet another portrait of the opioid epidemic, which continues to claim lives and devastate families at an escalating rate. Opioids, which are prescribed to control pain but are also highly addictive, dominate the statistics for drug overdose and deaths. In 2021, of the 107,000 drug overdose deaths reported (six times the number of overdose deaths in 1999), more than 75% involved an opioid.[1]

As the Centers for Disease Control and Prevention (CDC) explained in a policy report, "The unprecedented rise in overdose deaths in the US parallels a 300% increase since

1999 in the sale of these strong painkillers."[2] According to Johns Hopkins Medicine, one of the most respected medical institutions in the world, "About 75% of people in the U.S. who became addicted to street opioids such as heroin during the 2000s report that they started out taking prescription opioid drugs."[3] The issue is one of availability and cost: as prescription opioids become more difficult to obtain, a person who is addicted turns to other sources.

These facts are more than tragic statistics. Each data point is a human tragedy. The pain is felt deeply by family, friends, and communities. As the father of five adult children and grandfather of a new grandson, I cannot imagine the enormity of the losses these families experience not only at the time of a loved one's death but also for years afterwards as they try to understand what happened.

Cammie Wolf Rice, the smiling mother posing with her son in the photo, has lived with this pain for years. Yet, out of the depth of her anguish, she has found the emotional, physical, and spiritual strength to turn the loss of her son into a legacy of helping others. Today, she is CEO and founder of the Christopher Wolf Crusade, a nonprofit organization dedicated to greater education, awareness, and prevention of opioid addiction.

The use of the word *crusade* in the organization's name is particularly powerful because it describes the intensity of Cammie's mission. "I want to keep other mothers—other parents—from ever going through what I did."

CHRISTOPHER'S STORY

When I learned about the Christopher Wolf Crusade from one of my Kellogg MBA students, whom you'll meet later in this chapter, I was eager to meet with Cammie and her husband, John Rice, who was Christopher's stepfather and retired as vice chairman of GE.

Cammie and John described the work of the Christopher Wolf Crusade, including its latest efforts to bring more interventions to hospitals in rural communities where the opioid crisis is often the most severe. Yet, throughout our discussion, I did not view them as philanthropists and nonprofit organizers. I saw them as parents, first and foremost. Behind Cammie's smile and her hopeful words about scaling nationally, I saw the evidence of a grieving mother. Loss will always be the foundation of this legacy.

Cammie began her story in the late 1990s when Christopher was 13 years old and diagnosed with ulcerative colitis, a painful inflammatory bowel disease that affects the lining of the large intestine. The disease was so severe, most of Christopher's colon had to be removed when he was a senior in high school. He lost 75 days of school that year due to illness and had to miss his high school graduation.

Christopher soon had another health challenge, one that would ultimately cost him his life. During his hospitalization following his surgery, Christopher was prescribed opioid painkillers by his attending physician. Unbeknownst to his family or his doctors, even before Christopher left the hospital, he became addicted to opioids.

"That first prescription hijacked his brain," Cammie recalled. "We were following the doctor's orders—giving Christopher a pill every four hours. We went home with 90 OxyContin."

A narcotic, OxyContin (oxycodone hydrochloride) is prescribed for moderate to severe pain from surgery, injuries, and certain medical conditions. It is highly addictive.

Yet, in the 1990s and into the early 2000s, OxyContin and similar opioid painkillers were widely prescribed.[4] This was also the time of "pain as the fifth vital sign," a well-intended drive to improve patient health and comfort by addressing pain. The unintended consequence, however, was increased use of opioid painkillers and what has been called "overzealous" treatment of pain by some clinicians.[5]

This clinical background is necessary to understand what happened to Christopher when he was only a teenager. That first prescription started a battle with opioid addiction that lasted the rest of his life.

Like most young people, Christopher made plans for his future. He graduated from college with a finance degree but later decided his calling was elsewhere. That led him to pursue a master's degree in social work. Just knowing that detail, we can imagine this young man wanting to use his personal experiences to help others. That sense of purpose likely was shaped, at least in part, by the example of his family and their engagement in philanthropy. For example, Cammie and John are supporters of a community-based education facility in Cambodia known as The Rice Academy. Run by the Cambodian Children's Fund (CCF), the school opened in 2014 in one of the most impoverished areas of Phnom Penh and serves 200 children. Cammie is a long-time CCF supporter and serves on the US board of CCF.[6]

In 2016, while Cammie and John were overseas, Christopher traveled to Hong Kong to meet them; then Cammie and Christopher went to Cambodia. At some point on that trip, however, Christopher's addiction overcame him. He obtained heroin, which is frequently used by those who have become addicted to prescription opioids. His mother found him dead in the hotel bathroom.

"It took me two years to even say the word 'overdose,' even to my family," Cammie said. "I was like a zombie living in a surreal world."

During those two years, Cammie suffered more losses. Her mother passed away, and her brother died after taking a Xanax he'd bought from a dealer, which had been laced with fentanyl. Her brother's death reflects another aspect of the opioid crisis. Dealers frequently put fentanyl into the drugs they sell to make them highly addictive; even a small amount of fentanyl can result in overdose or death.

Processing these compounding losses led Cammie to an emotional crossroads. She could choose to stay locked in her grief and anger at the health care profession and the pharmaceutical industry, especially certain drug companies that initially had marketed opioids as safe for patients experiencing pain.[7] Or, she could channel her grief into a quest to understand how this had happened to Christopher. She chose the latter, which led Cammie on a path of engaging and partnering with the health care system. She was motivated by one goal: help break the stigma about opioid addiction to promote prevention.

Speaking Up and Speaking Out

In the case of opioid addiction, there is often a stigma that it happens to "other people" and their families. It is a form of denial, but with judgment that is insensitive and ultimately dehumanizing.

Blinded by this attitude, people refuse to see the warning signs of addiction in their loved ones or try to hide their own behaviors, instead of seeking help. Yet, the statistics tell another story. A 2018 national poll by the American Psychiatric Association found that nearly a third of Americans say they knew someone who is or had been addicted to opioids or prescription painkillers.[8] To bring the point home further, the CDC states that opioid addiction can "affect anyone—regardless of race, gender, income level, or social class. Like many other medical conditions, evidence-based treatments are available . . . but seeking treatment remains stigmatized. Stigma can be a major barrier to how well prevention and treatment programs work against the opioid crisis."

Cammie recognized that she could help shatter the silence that acts as a barrier to prevention and intervention. Public speaking, however, was not something she was naturally drawn to, and speaking about her son's death would make it doubly uncomfortable. As a first step, Cammie sought out coaching from a woman who had lost three children and yet found the courage to keep speaking out. "She told me, 'Turn that pain into purpose!' The more I did that, the better I felt. It was a fire inside me."

Cammie reached out to doctors to learn more about addiction, particularly cases like Christopher's that began with a prescription given for pain. "So much addiction begins in the hospital. Young people who suffer a football injury go home with a big bottle of pills," Cammie said.

The more Cammie talked—including conversations with more than 150 medical professionals—the more urgency she felt about reaching a wider audience. That led her to write a book in which she shares her personal story—*The Flight: My Opioid Journey.* Quickly, the book became a way to connect with others and allow them to also speak out about their own losses, as well as their paths to healing and recovery. As one reader who described herself as "a Registered Nurse and as a parent of a daughter who died from Fentanyl poisoning" wrote in an online review, "It is painful to read of her [Cammie's] journey through the opioid crisis, but it has been the most healing experience for me as a grieving mother."[9]

The Missing Pieces

Early on in their fact-finding mission about opioid use and abuse, John and Cammie made a startling discovery: addiction was largely absent in most medical school curricula at the time. In other words, doctors-in-training weren't being educated about the complexities of addiction to prescription pain medication. As the opioid crisis has revealed, even when prescribed according to stringent guidelines, painkillers can lead to dependency and addiction—and potentially overdose and death.

John voiced his frustration over what he learned from a former dean of a medical school about why opioid addiction has been largely absent in the curriculum. "He said to me, 'The accrediting bodies don't give us any credit for it.' Medical school students have to know every bone in the foot, even though they are not going to be involved in podiatry or orthopedics, but they don't learn about opioid addiction."

John's assertion is backed by what researchers have found in their reviews of medical school curricula in the United States: a need to integrate chronic pain and opioid addiction and assessment tools into curricula.[10] The American Medical Association has spoken out on the topic as well in its 2021 "Overdose Epidemic Report." It cites conflicting statistics that point to the complexity of this epidemic. On the one hand, there has been a 44% decrease in the number of opioid painkiller prescriptions written between 2011 and 2020; on the other hand, drug overdoses continue to occur with rising numbers of deaths. In addition, "Millions with a substance use disorder remain without access to evidence-based care."[11] (One hopeful example is Rosalind Franklin University's Chicago Medical School. It was honored in 2023 for its collaboration with GPF Foundation on a medical simulation educational tool that is designed to help frontline medical providers improve diagnosis and treatment of patients experiencing adverse effects of psycho-stimulants, such as cocaine.)[12]

Given the breadth and depth of the opioid crisis, it can only be tackled with multiple strategies, including more education, intervention, and treatment. This includes expanding access to naloxone (often known by its trade name, Narcan, which is available over the counter) to reverse overdoses. For its part, the Christopher Wolf Crusade channels its energy into prevention—in other words, stopping opioid addiction before it takes hold.

A significant step forward in this mission occurred as the Christopher Wolf Crusade was being launched. Cammie attended a conference where one of the speakers was Dr. Mara Schenker, an orthopedic trauma surgeon whose many titles include associate professor and chief of orthopedics at Grady Memorial Hospital and director of orthopedic trauma for Emory University. After her presentation Cammie walked up to Mara, acting on an intuition that this was exactly the right person with whom to engage. An instant connection was made, and soon Mara accepted the invitation to volunteer as chief medical officer of the Christopher Wolf Crusade.

Enter a Champion in the Crusade's Cause

The story shifts at this point to Mara Schenker who, coincidentally, was one of my students in Kellogg's Executive MBA program in 2023. After receiving her undergraduate degree in neuroscience from the University of Pittsburgh, Mara entered medical school at the University of Chicago and became an orthopedic trauma surgeon. That led her to taking a job with Emory University and its Grady Memorial Hospital, located in downtown Atlanta. The only Level 1 trauma center in Atlanta, it is also the biggest in the country. This professional background alone would have made Mara a valuable partner in expanding the work of the Christopher Wolf Crusade. But, as so often happens when connections occur, there were more commonalities behind the scene.

Mara shared with me a little more of her personal story and those who influenced her, starting with her parents. Her father, who passed away in February 2023, had served in the Air Force and then became a CPA. After working as an accountant for 10 years, he was forced into retirement because of multiple sclerosis. He was in a wheelchair since Mara was seven, and her mother was his caregiver for 35 years. "But Dad never complained a day in his life. He had the greatest attitude," Mara recalled. "And that impacted everything I've ever done. I don't complain. If there is a problem I face, let me figure out how to solve it."

As a young athlete, Mara took up Taekwondo, the Korean martial art, and was a 2001 world champion. "I had thought I would do that forever, then I got injured." As she considered what to do next, Mara decided on orthopedics. She recalled her medical school training in the 2000s. "Back then, the opioid crisis was gaining a lot of traction, but not a lot of awareness. As residents, we would routinely give patients 120 pain pills when they were discharged—that was the standard."

As she went into practice, Mara wanted to learn more about opioid prescription best practices. When she asked a colleague how her own prescription practices compared to those of her peers, Mara was shocked by what she learned. "I was told, 'You are the person who is most willing to re-prescribe,'" Mara recalled. "I was not trained on addiction medicine. I was not trained on how to manage a patient's pain other than to give them a pill."

That led Mara to deepen her understanding of pain and pain management, which differs greatly from patient to patient. "Every person's manifestation of pain is different— and every person's risk of addiction is different," Mara explained.

Another nuance is setting expectations about pain. Some pain after a severe injury or complex surgery is to be expected. Trying to completely eradicate pain can lead to overuse of painkillers, thus increasing the risk of addiction.

Mara began speaking at medical conferences about her own experience prescribing opioids. It was at one such event that she met Cammie. "She was sitting in the audience and came up to me afterwards," Mara recalled. "She said to me, 'I appreciate your honesty. Would you like to have lunch with me?'"

The two of them had an immediate connection and joined forces from their unique perspectives: Cammie as a bereaved mother and advocate, and Mara as a physician. "We've come together to explore how we can better support patients," Mara said.

Together, they are partnering in the next phase of inter-vention undertaken by the Christopher Wolf Crusade—one that has the potential to make a significant difference in the education and support of patients in managing their pain.

A New Solution: The Life Care Specialist

Taking a step back, we can appreciate that had Cammie decided only to share her personal story, she would have provided support to other families affected by their loved ones' addictions and deaths by overdose. After all, she is not a medical professional by training. Cammie easily could have left it to others—"experts" whom we expect to have all the answers—to change the way health care systems address pain. But Cammie didn't stop there.

Given her network, resources, and conviction to make a difference, Cammie has broken new ground through the Christopher Wolf Crusade. Specifically, the organization is funding pilot programs for a health care position known as a life care specialist. Trained in evidence-based behavioral techniques, life care specialists can support patients by teach-ing them alternative techniques for managing pain, as well as helping identify their risk of opioid dependence.

When I asked Cammie how this idea came about, she described a previous experience that provided some inspira-tion. When children are diagnosed with serious illnesses or chronic conditions, particularly those requiring lengthy hos-pital stays, they often work with child life specialists. These professionals provide emotional support to young patients and coping strategies for families. Once children pass the age of 18, however, such assistance is no longer available.

Cammie was convinced that this type of support was exactly what patients experiencing pain from trauma need.

She tested the idea with senior health care leaders, particularly at Emory, where she had the most contact, and was told that nothing like the life care specialist concept existed. In addition, the dean of Emory's nursing school embraced the idea saying, "We need it, but we don't know how to pay for it."

One of the major challenges is that insurance companies do not pay for the services provided by the life care specialists because there is no approved billing code. Having a code that would allow for that payment would be the holy grail for this whole program, enabling it to be scaled across all health care systems. Rather than being discouraged by a lack of funding, the Christopher Wolf Crusade found another way. The organization self-funded a pilot program at Grady Memorial Hospital, with Mara leading the clinical trial.

The pilot program at Grady started with one life care specialist, and then expanded to three. The life care specialists developed rapport with nurses on the hospital floor who often have heavy caseloads of trauma patients. When a patient continually complains of unbearable pain, nursing staff has no time to coach them in pain management techniques; the response is often to give the next dose of opioid medication.

This is where life care specialists can help fill the gap. They work with individual patients to assess their understanding of the medications they're being prescribed and teach them alternative therapies, such as exercises, meditation, music therapy, and other techniques that shift the focus away from the experience of pain. "They are all brain distractions—to take the brain away from where the pain is," Cammie said.

Although they are trained to work alongside health care teams, the life care specialists are not required to have a clinical background. This enables hospitals to recruit from within the community. Among those applying for these positions are first responders such as firefighters and emergency medical technicians, as well as those who have an interest in addiction intervention and alternative therapies for managing pain. To ensure they are well trained, the Christopher Wolf Crusade, in partnership with Mercer University School of Medicine, has developed a curriculum to certify its life care specialists, who also receive on-the-job training in the hospitals. Life care specialists are also certified in evidence-based skills to help patients manage their anxiety, depression, and post-traumatic stress disorder. They use a risk-assessment tool to help identify those at greatest risk for addiction. Life care specialists also follow up with patients post-discharge.

The life care specialists not only make a difference in the lives of the patients they serve but also have the potential to save money for the hospitals where they work. The savings stem from helping keep patients from returning to the emergency department for pain. Under insurance guidelines, if a patient who has been discharged from the hospital returns within 30 days, the insurance company will not pay for that additional emergency department treatment or hospitalization. It is a significant financial penalty for hospitals and health systems.

Opioid misuse and overdose can result in trauma patients returning to the hospital within that 30-day window. "If even two patients do not come back to the hospital you have paid for the life care specialist position for a year," Cammie said.

The pilot program at Grady Memorial has been successful, and the program now services patients in sickle cell, orthopedic trauma, and palliative care units and, as of this writing, is moving into oncology. The program is also expanding to Emory Midtown hospital.

Building on these positive results, the Christopher Wolf Crusade is introducing life care specialists in six hospitals in rural Georgia, thanks to a $1 million grant from a private foundation. The target is rural health care facilities because these areas are often affected by high rates of opioid misuse, overdose, and death. For the first two years, the grant will pay for two specialists at each hospital; after that time, the hospitals are expected to fund the positions.

In addition, a $200,000 grant will support Emory and the Christopher Wolf Crusade in their work with sports injury patients. Another source may come from the states receiving settlement money in the cases brought against opioid drug manufacturers by the US Justice Department. John and Cammie hope that, as the life care specialists prove their value, states will channel a portion of their settlement money into such prevention programs. With opioid settlement funding, they are currently launching in three rural hospitals in Arkansas.

"We need a big horse to ride if we want to scale nationally," Cammie said. "But not too big of a horse. We need to work with [health systems] that really care about rural communities. We want to be successful at rural first."

A Tireless Journey

At the end of our conversation, Cammie made a joke that talking with her and John about the Christopher Wolf Crusade was like drinking out of a firehose. But that is precisely what makes this legacy so powerful. Within a few short years, Cammie turned her immeasurable grief into the conviction that something can and must be done to break the cycle of opioid addiction. This is the kind of commitment that inspires accolades. And yet, we cannot lose sight of the fact that the progress made by the Christopher Wolf Crusade started with the untimely, tragic death of a young man.

"Sometimes people say to Cammie or to me, 'Are you better now? Are you feeling better?' But after losing a child, you don't get well—you just deal with it. So many people don't understand that," John said.

In the next breath, though, he emphasized the therapeutic benefit of engaging in this work. It combines all the intensity involved in any startup organization, with a very personal purpose that is reinforced with every conversation Cammie has with other parents who have lost a child to opioid addiction.

"I am working harder now than I ever did in the corporate world," Cammie said. "But when I get a call or a text from a mom who is going through this—or we have a success story of the life care specialists—I know I have to keep going. I'm helping people I don't even know. What else would I be doing?"

A LASTING LEGACY

At any age the loss of a child is profoundly painful. Research shows that the death of a child triggers enduring grief, even more intense than what is experienced with the passing of a spouse or a parent.[13] The bereaved parents face an existential crisis: *Why did God let this happen? Children should outlive their parents!*

Among those who study grief, an important milestone in living with grief occurs at 13 months. After the end of the first year and a month, those who are mourning have completed the cycle of grieving through holidays, birthdays, and other significant events. The pain in the second year often is not as strong, but it remains and will be with the person for the rest of their lives, experts in grief state. For parents who lost a child, though, that grieving process could very well extend far longer—perhaps even the rest of their lives. After such a profound loss, there may not be closure—the parents and other family members are forever changed. And yet, life does go on.

When I talked to my good friend Dr. Daven Morrison, an organizational psychiatrist, about how parents can find a way to move on from tragic loss, he mentioned the importance of reframing. This process honors one's feelings of loss by turning them into intention and action. As Cammie said previously, sharing the advice she received, "Turn that pain into purpose!"

In honor of a deceased child or other loved one, a family might sponsor a community fundraiser such as a 5K run or a walk-a-thon for a good cause—one that is particularly meaningful to them. I'm reminded of a 5K race and a 1-mile fun run held many years ago in the Chicago area, organized by Monte Briner, who suffered from amyotrophic lateral sclerosis, or Lou Gehrig's disease. I knew him during my days as CEO of Baxter. Miles for Monte was held for nine years while Monte was alive and then one last event he planned to be held after death in 1998. In total, more than $900,000 was raised for ALS research.[14] A few years later, Monte's family brought back the fundraiser.

In the same way, endowments and other charitable donations can be made in the name of the deceased. For example, a child who died while in high school is honored with a scholarship that helps other students pursue their futures. By giving to others, the person's name lives on through good works. "It offers a kind of 'immortality' for the person who died, in the context of creating meaning and actions," Daven explained.

At family gatherings, we honor our loved one's memory as we tell our favorite stories, recalling the love, laughter, and connection we shared. We may engage in rituals—releasing a balloon on the anniversary of our loved one's death or planting flowers at their grave each spring. Tricia Crisafulli, who has helped in the writing of this and my previous books, described how each winter she goes cross-country skiing around the anniversary of the death of her sister Bernadette (who also loved the sport). Along the trail, Tricia picks a spot of unblemished snow to write her sister's name with the tip of her ski pole and says a prayer.

Then there are the truly remarkable actions, such as the Christopher Wolf Crusade, through which Cammie has channeled her loss into positive change. No matter that each speech she gives, each conversation she engages in, recalls the enormity of losing her son, Christopher. She relives that pain in order to reach out and connect with others—with help and hope to prevent more deaths from opioid overdose.

Courage is too small a word, and conviction doesn't capture the selflessness involved. Perhaps the best word is *love*—the only force powerful enough to turn loss into legacy.

- *How can we honor our loved ones as we establish and build a legacy?*
- *What philanthropic causes did they champion?*
- *How can we keep the memory of them alive as we give of ourselves?*

CHAPTER 6

WHO ARE "THOSE GUYS"?

"To whom much is given, much will be required."

—*Luke 12:48*

Too often, when people consider all the problems in the world—poverty, hunger, injustice, inequality, disparity in access to health care, and so many more—they look around to see who will step up and solve them. For years, in my classes at Kellogg about becoming a values-based leader, I will ask the students whom they expect will deal with all these problems. Almost every time, the assumption is that someone else will do it. And everybody refers to these people by the same name: "those guys," a gender-neutral term for people with money, power, and influence.

It's true that some of the world's wealthiest and most influential people do engage in philanthropy. They start foundations and donate to charity and causes. But just because someone on the *Forbes* billionaire's list is also a philanthropist does not mean that we can or should rely on that person to do all the work. If we want to live in a better world, we cannot wait for someone else to step up to the challenge. It's up to us.

Or, as I tell both students in my classes at Kellogg and the executives and professionals who attend my talks, presentations, and seminars: *Guess what? We are those guys!*

This line always gets a smile or a laugh, whether I'm speaking to a group of students or to 500 executives at a Fortune 100 company. And there's no mistaking the meaning. All of us are those guys. If people like us are not going to deal with these issues, then who the heck is? And when it comes to leaving a legacy of helping to change the world, once again, *we are those guys.*

It's like that safety reminder we see in train stations, airports, and other public places: "If you see something, say something." Our mantra could be, "If you see something, *do* something."

Throughout this book thus far, we've heard from many people who are making a difference. Clearly, they are "those guys." In this chapter, we'll take it a step further by sharing stories of those who, in their daily lives, realized that they could truly make a difference. For each of them, there was a moment—an epiphany combined with an opportunity—to do something specific that could help change the world. They saw what needed to be done—and they started doing something about it.

The four people profiled in this chapter are at various stages of their lives. One is a young entrepreneur, striving to scale her nonprofit social enterprise. Another is an award-winning television broadcaster with a mission to improve equity, access, and well-being in her community. Two others have had long careers and are now engaged in projects that will be of significant importance in certain parts of the world.

By these varied examples we are reminded, once again, that making a difference does not require wealth, a certain title, or even many decades of life experience. All we have to do is show up and say yes.

STEPHEN ISAACS: FROM WORLD WANDERER TO WORLD CHANGER

I have known Stephen Isaacs for more than 30 years. We first got to know each other as health care industry colleagues. At the time, I was chairman and CEO of Baxter International, and Steve was president and CEO of Cerus Corporation, a biomedical products company that developed systems to safeguard blood products and blood used in transfusions. Later, Steve founded Aduro Biotech, focused on immuno-oncology (a form of cancer treatment), autoimmunity, and infectious disease; he was chairman, president, and CEO from 2008 to 2020. Steve is still active in biotech, such as a startup developing new antibiotics to fight drug-resistant microbes and pathogens. Anyone who has ever heard or read about the dangers of "superbugs"—bacteria, viruses, and other pathogens that are resistant to most of the antibiotics and other medications used to treat the infections they cause—will understand the importance of this new company's mission. Believe me when I tell you: the legacy Steve is creating through this latest venture is its research—not the profit it could possibly generate one day. He's also an advisor to Yemaachi Biotech, the first biotech company founded in Ghana, which is searching for cancer markers within the genetically diverse African population.

Steve Isaacs totes a sack of grain.
Source: Courtesy of Steve Isaacs.

  Reading this—knowing my background and now Steve's—you might conclude that our common ground is health care. But that's only partially true. As it turns out, Steve and I both share a commitment to doing what we can to make a difference in the lives of people in Africa. My activities are supporting One Acre Fund and its life-changing assistance to smallholder farmers in Africa, which you'll read about in Chapter 7. Steve is more boots-on-the-ground, with various projects and humanitarian endeavors in several African countries, including Kenya, Malawi, Uganda, and Zimbabwe.

I'm proud to call Steve my friend and to say, without question, that he is hardwired for change. Steve is a traveler who has allowed his wanderings to open his eyes to the beauty of the world. He forges connections and builds relationships with people whose lives appear so different from his. And when he sees a problem—in health care, education, or nutrition—he finds a way to address it.

In looking back on his early influences, Steve recalled a high school biology teacher in Concord, California, who had attended the University of California at Berkeley—and had a beard. "He was the talk of the school for that beard," Steve said. "And I liked the idea that he didn't conform. Conformity and blind obedience have always seemed very boring to me, and I often got myself in trouble for these views and for having a defiant tongue."

Steve vividly remembers the day when this teacher showed his class slides of a trip he'd taken to Afghanistan—exploring the desert, walking under the stars, meeting shepherds out in the wilds alone, sleeping in Bedouin tents . . . "At age 14, this sparked my imagination, and I realized that there was a big world out there beyond the confines of Concord, California. I knew I would somehow have to see it."

This spark of curiosity motivated Steve to explore the world—Nepal, India, Bhutan, Indonesia, China, Thailand, Brazil, and several African countries. After he married and had children, Steve took his two daughters on those travels, starting with a trip to China when they were ages one and three. "From a young age, it became very apparent to them that most of the world doesn't live in the same way they do. The disparity of life was also laid wide open to them," Steve said. "They learned a lot about empathy—and the desire to give back followed. It has made a real difference in their lives—and in mine as well."

What happened to Steve and his family is a transition from world wanderers—people who explore for the adventure—to world changers. For them, it isn't enough to meet people and experience interesting cultures in faraway places. Steve and his family get to know the people—their joy and celebrations, their struggles and sorrows. And where there is a need and help is welcomed, they find a way to become involved with humanitarian projects in partnership with local people. They avoid imposing solutions to problems that outsiders don't fully understand (a behavior we'll also discuss in Chapter 7).

Steve and his family are also careful not to perpetuate the problems of "voluntourism," which has been criticized for sending volunteers from rich nations to low-income countries for a few weeks of acting out "white savior complex" and rescuer behavior.[1] Steve and his family have a long-term, deep commitment to Africa. He travels to Kenya three to four times a year, and more recently also spends time in Malawi, where he is supporting the quail farm profiled in Chapter 4. With each trip, he builds new relationships and strengthens existing ones, while furthering his understanding of the needs and priorities of the people he meets.

I asked Steve to explain how he came to appreciate the importance of getting to know the people he wants to help. In response, he shared a story about an experience that had the opposite effect. It was 1993, and Steve took his family (including his daughters, ages three and five at the time) on a luxury safari with all the amenities. "The point was to see the animals, not interact with the people. The guide treated the local people almost as an extension of the elephants and lions, and he made sure we did not get too close," Steve recalled.

That experience was precisely what he did *not* want for himself or his family. On the next trip to Kenya, they skipped "the fancy travel company and the overly protective guide," and instead did a 10-day walking tour with the Samburu warriors in Kenya's Northern Frontier District. That first walk with the Samburu was not the last for Steve; in 2022, he took another 100-mile walk with them.

In summer 2004, Steve's daughters, who were 14 and 16, went to Kenya on their own to teach fourth grade at a school in Kasigau. From that experience, these young women founded the ABE (A Better Education) Club in Kasigau. Out of the original ABE Club, the Isaacs's family foundation has grown to support the education of several hundred students, from preschool through university. The foundation also built a health care clinic in 2015 and trained the medical officer who runs it. Other projects receiving foundation support include microfinancing activities and a student lunch program that feeds about 1,800 youth every day.

Steve's philanthropic endeavors are numerous—frankly, too many to list here. For example, he is supporting the building of Kenyatta National Hospital's Hope Hostel, a three-story facility that will provide free accommodation and food to cancer patients. His other activities include being on the board of the Center for Global Development in Washington, DC; a trustee of the UC Berkeley Foundation; and a trustee of UC Berkeley's Blum Center for Developing Economies, where he helps raise funds for students from

Ghana, Kenya, Nigeria, and Malawi to study for a master of development engineering degree.

It's a long list—and might even reinforce the impression that to make a difference you need to be a CEO with a world-wide network and the resources to go with it. Steve, however, quickly debunks that impression. For him, it simply comes down to doing whatever you can—and wherever you are. "You don't need to go to Kenya to make an impact," he said. "You can sign up to be a mentor in your community. Give your time instead of money."

At this stage of his life, Steve remains committed to doing all he can for the communities he cares deeply about, particularly the people of Kasigau. But he acknowledges the complexity of the needs of that community. "They are endless, and they keep growing—education, health care, nutrition, water problems caused by a four-year drought . . .," he said. "It's difficult to meet all the funding challenges and to spend the amount of time that's required to keep it all going. The focus is sometimes hard to maintain as well, given all the other activities that are going on."

Despite the challenges, this world wanderer has no plans to stop his travels or his involvement. In fact, just recently, Steve was handing out sacks of maize in Kenya when he saw a little girl, standing with her mother. This child was about the same age as his own granddaughter back in California, and he was instantly struck by the contrast. His granddaughter has never been without food; her parents do not worry about where their next meal will come from. But this little girl in a tattered dress and broken shoes knew hunger.

"So, we are sponsoring her now," he said. "Maybe that's problematic—one child out of so many. But I had to do something for her."

That is a risk of being one of those guys. You can't just rely on your intellect and your expertise. It takes heart—not only to see another person's need, but also to feel it.

From my personal faith perspective, I would also add that we are all children of God. And if we do not help our brothers and sisters who live everywhere on this planet, then what are we doing with our lives?

MAZIWA: HELPING MOTHERS AND THEIR BABIES

It looked like a dream job and one with the potential to make an impact. Sahar Jamal was working for Johnson & Johnson, the global pharmaceutical company, as a senior brand manager, in Toronto and the UK, and also involved in the company's corporate social responsibility (CSR) activities.

Having grown up in Vancouver, British Columbia, Sahar already had a global perspective, thanks to her father, who was from Tanzania, and her mother, who was from India. Through her job at J&J, including as the CSR lead in the UK, she had become deeply interested in global health issues, particularly those affecting women and children, but she wanted to do more.

Sahar left J&J to pursue an MBA at Kellogg, where she also led the Social Impact Club. Given her passion for global health, Sahar chose an internship with Jacaranda Health in Kenya. Jacaranda follows a model of partnership, working closely with government agencies to improve the quality of care and outcomes for mothers and their infants.

While at Jacaranda Health, Sahar met hundreds of mothers who were struggling to find a way to continue breastfeeding their babies while they worked. The issue was not that the women needed to be convinced about the importance of breastfeeding, which provides health benefits for both mother and child. (The Centers for Disease Control and Prevention calls it the "clinical gold standard for infant feeding and nutrition.")[2] In fact, all the well-intentioned attempts by outside organizations to educate women in Kenya about the importance of breastfeeding only served to shame them about what they were not doing for their babies.

By listening to the women, Sahar gained insight into their struggles. "Their problem was they were torn between having to stay at home to breastfeed their infants and returning to work to support their families," Sahar explained. "Often, these women were spending one hour a day commuting to work, putting in a 10-hour workday, and then commuting another hour back home. They said to me, 'How am I supposed to breastfeed my baby when my family needs my income?'"

After speaking with hundreds of Kenyan mothers, Sahar learned that the answer was in finding a way for these women to express their milk to feed their babies while they were at work. Most breast pumps available to women, however, operated manually and were often ineffective. Electric pumps improved convenience and effectiveness; however, in Kenya, these breast pumps were often expensive and bulky to carry. What these women needed was a practical tool. This inspired Sahar to establish Maziwa, which means *milk* in Swahili. Her idea was to launch a discreet, portable, and low-cost breast pump and disseminate practical lactation support through a network of community ambassadors.

What's important to understand is that Sahar's advocacy for women in Kenya had nothing to do with personal experience. She is not a mother herself and has no family ties to Kenya. Rather, as one of those guys, she encountered a problem which needed addressing and made that mission a reality.

During her second year at Kellogg, Sahar was chosen for the Zell Fellowship Program, a competitive accelerator program for MBA students. Through a multidisciplinary class called NUvention, Sahar was teamed with a doctor, a lawyer, and an engineer to develop a prototype breast pump. In 2019, she was named Kellogg's Social Entrepreneur of the Year. Maziwa received several awards and raised seed capital from MIT SOLVE and the Gates Foundation.

With such a promising start, Sahar moved to Kenya in 2019. Then COVID hit, and the pandemic led to shutdowns around the world. Sahar moved back to Vancouver and into her parents' basement. Despite the setback, she did not stop—she merely shifted gears, from rolling out the initial product to doing more fundraising. By 2021, with funding in place, Sahar returned to Kenya. Her Kenyan team, based in and around Nairobi, is composed of seven people from a variety of backgrounds—marketing, sales, finance, community engagement, customer service, and quality assurance— who have been working part-time so far, to stretch their lean budget.

"Fundraising capacity is our biggest constraint," Sahar said. "We have only scratched the surface of the market in Kenya."

Over the past two years, Maziwa has doubled its sales without increasing its budget. Maziwa's Community Breastfeeding Ambassadors have helped increase demand and expand the organization's reach to new counties in Kenya. But there are so many more women and infants who could benefit from their work. Expanding Maziwa's impact and reach will also drive sustainability, as higher volumes bring economies of scale; this will allow the organization to break even while supporting a strong full-time team.

The trade-off, as Sahar explained, is one of breadth versus depth. Breadth would take Maziwa into more countries, but depth would increase engagement with more users in one large market. At the moment, Sahar is more focused on the latter, ensuring that women in Kenya are given education and support as they are introduced to the product, and experience a difference in their lives. At the same time, she realizes that Maziwa has a solution to a problem facing women everywhere. In the next five years, Maziwa's expansion plans target Rwanda, Tanzania, Uganda, and potentially South Africa.

"I believe this need exists all around the world—across Africa, as well as in Southeast Asia and Latin America," Sahar said. "Our vision is to scale strategically as far as we can to new geographies and expand our network of ambassadors that go beyond our organization. We will equip grassroots leaders in new markets who can provide lactation support to women in the community."

Without question, Sahar is on a far different path than her career trajectory would have been had she stayed at Johnson & Johnson. One obvious difference is she would be earning far more money at J&J, while making some contribution through its CSR activities. But that wasn't enough for Sahar. She wanted to make a significant impact—or, as she explained it, "I wanted to make sure I was directly making a difference in the lives of women."

For her, that is the ultimate calling.

MACEDONIA2025: FOR LOVE
OF THE HOMELAND

In the first two stories, we met people who address the needs of people in other parts of the world where they developed deep connections. For others, however, the desire to make a difference takes them back to their roots. That is the story of Macedonia2025 and one of its cofounders, my friend Mike Zafirovski.

Mike was born in the city of Skopje, in what was then the Socialist Federal Republic of Yugoslavia, and which today is the capital of the Republic of Macedonia (officially known as North Macedonia). In 1969, when Mike was 15, he immigrated to the United States with his family. They arrived in Cleveland, Ohio, speaking no English and with a total of $1,500. Two years later—after switching from soccer, which he had played growing up, to swimming—Mike went to college on a swimming scholarship.

"Having grown up in a communist country, it took a while for me to really start feeling like an American. But eventually, like most immigrants before me, I embraced democracy, free enterprise, and the American way of life," Mike said.

Through hard work and determination, Mike experienced the American dream. He rose through the ranks of General Electric and then held top leadership positions at Motorola. Later, he became CEO of Nortel and executive advisor at Blackstone.

As his professional career advanced at Motorola, Mike received another opportunity—this time, from Macedonia President Boris Trajkovski, who led the country from 1999 until his tragic death in a plane crash in 2004. President Trajkovski expressed his pride for everything this Macedonian

American executive had achieved; then he asked Mike to put his business acumen to work for his homeland. Two weeks later, Mike was in Macedonia for discussions with the president and his staff. Among Mike's achievements were eventually convincing Motorola to install its WiMAX broadband in Macedonia and President Trajkovski and his staff to start pursuing foreign investments in an organized way.

A few years later, in 2006, then Prime Minister Branko Crvenkovski was in Canada, making a direct appeal to the Macedonian diaspora for ideas of how to help Macedonia's economic growth and its fledgling democracy. After the prime minister's speech, Mike heard someone in the room call his name.

The man was John Bitove Sr., a Macedonian Canadian businessman and philanthropist, whom Mike called his "role model and hero." John Sr. then turned to the prime minister and said, "You want ideas on how to make your country stronger? Here are the two men who can help you make that happen."

Those two people were Mike Zafirovski and John Bitove Jr., John Sr.'s son.

"How do you say no to someone and something like that?" Mike said. "And that was the genesis of what became Macedonia2025."

Officially founded in 2007, Macedonia2025 began as a small group and "stayed mostly under the radar" at first, as Mike explained. Since then, the organization has grown in scope and vision. Today, it has a 20-member board of directors, a larger advisory board, and a growing "Ambassadors Club" composed of professionals of Macedonian origin around the world, who volunteer to assist with the organization's ambitious projects and events.

Macedonia2025 describes itself as an "international, independent, nonpolitical 'think and do' tank." That description, itself, captures the essence of being those guys. Rather than being a think tank that analyzes problems and recommends possible solutions, Macedonia2025 puts the emphasis on *do*—in particular, to enable expatriates to give back to their homeland, which has many economic, social, and governance needs.

Doing the Right Thing—and the Best They Can

Over the past few years, I've had the pleasure of being a guest speaker on values-based leadership at Macedonia2025 meetings in Skopje and, most recently, in Florida. What always impresses me about this group is the lack of personal agenda on the part of the Macedonia2025 team. Their motivation goes to the heart of what values-based leadership is all about: striving to do the right thing and the best they can. The beneficiaries of their efforts will be the 2 million people in their homeland, and the generations who follow.

"We take our role very seriously being those guys. We *should* make a significant impact," Mike said. "A strong, independent, democratic Macedonia will be good for the citizens, for the region, and for the world. In the core of my being, I believe that."

Although Macedonia2025 relies on the commitment of many, it draws on the heart and soul of one man: John Bitove Sr., who died in 2015. In a tribute video posted on YouTube, John Sr. explained his life philosophy: "I always felt those who give will receive, as long as they do it with their heart. My mother was a very big believer in that . . . and to this day, I've said it many times to my children. And I say it to different people all the time."[3]

When it comes to giving, John Sr. left a remarkable legacy of philanthropy as a "proud Macedonia descendent." In return, he received the support, friendship, and partnership of many others for having lived a life of purpose. John Sr. was honored with the Order of Canada, the nation's highest honor for people making a significant contribution, as well as the September 8th Medal of Honor from Macedonia, named after its Independence Day.

His lasting legacy is Macedonia2025, dedicated to the economic development of the homeland. As his son and Macedonia2025 cofounder John Bitove Jr. told the *Toronto Star*, "It's part of the mantle we have to carry."[4]

Macedonia2025 focuses on four areas, which it calls *pillars*. The first is accelerating the competitiveness and growth of Macedonian businesses, including startups, and helping them enter foreign markets. The second is expanding leadership development, particularly among young, talented Macedonians. Progress on this pillar has been remarkable: training more than 1,000 managers, including 40 destined to be CEOs in Macedonia. The third is building strong partnerships worldwide and forging links within a global community of people of Macedonian origin and descent. The fourth is improving the country's business environment, such as eliminating political corruption and creating conditions in which businesses can thrive and foreign investment can be increased.

Eliminating corruption could be considered a fifth pillar, and it is one of the most crucial for Macedonia to establish the governance needed to assure foreign investors about doing business in the country. To put the problem in perspective, in an April 2023 report, the United States Agency for International Development, stated, "Corruption in North

Macedonia continues to erode trust in institutions, weakens accountability and transparency, obstructs economic growth, and contributes to political fragility and instability."[5] Ending corruption is also a prerequisite for another long-term goal championed by Macedonia2025: membership in the European Union. Even more important, achieving this goal will build Macedonians' confidence in the country and its institutions.

Rebranding a Country

Macedonia2025's CEO, Nikica Mojsoska Blazhevski, is an academic who has served as the dean of the School of Business Economics and Management at the University American Skopje in Macedonia. "By executing great programs, we can influence not just the economy and business but also the political sphere and society," she said. "We are ready, and we have the strength and resources as an organization. And where things are beyond our scope and resources, we try to inspire, motivate, and support."

The structural changes Macedonia2025 envisions will require partnership with both business and government. At the time of our conversation in March 2024, Macedonia was facing both presidential and parliamentary elections. Macedonia2025 prepared an ambitious "One Vision for Accelerated Growth" document, calling for unanimous consensus on the "path to prosperity" among the country's four major political parties and coalitions, academia, and the business community.

"We have big plans ahead of us. We want to influence and also support the new government," Nikica said.

Macedonia2025 also engages with the diaspora, such as with networking events held in various locations around the world, as well as its annual summit that brings together business leaders, entrepreneurs, investors, and policymakers. The agenda for the latest summit included topics not only relevant to the future of Macedonia but also to business and economic development around the globe: digitalization, strategic leadership, eliminating corruption, the future of work, supply chain resilience, and leveraging the capabilities of artificial intelligence and machine learning.

When Nikica talks about her vision of the future for Macedonia, she adds a word that resonates deeply for her: *rebranding*. By that, she means changing how the world perceives the country where she lives and works. "There is much work for us to be done, and it's a big word for us—*rebranding* the country," Nikica said.

Mike agreed, adding: "People expect more of the country. There is an opportunity for us to frame the issues and the opportunity. If they look at the messages [of Macedonia2025] how can they argue against economic growth or smart regulations, or fighting corruption?"

The legacy of Macedonia2025 will be what the country achieves as it evolves, hopefully into a democracy that supports entrepreneurship and economic growth to benefit all. That legacy, however, does not end with Macedonia. It also applies to inspiring people of other nationalities around the globe. To explain, Mike recalled speaking at a McKinsey conference in 2007 on global leadership and mentioning Macedonia2025's startup efforts during the question-and-answer period. After his speech, three McKinsey partners approached him—not to learn more about global leadership, but to provide advice from their own initiative for their homeland of Armenia. Mike was more than happy to engage with them and to apply their lessons learned to Macedonia2025's efforts. In turn, he and Macedonia2025 have been helpful to startup initiatives in several European and African countries.

"If you have a burning passion to do this work anywhere, be open. Try to see who else is doing it. Learn what is the best way," Mike added. "And, of course, be open to sharing. To whom much is given, much is expected—especially sharing with others."

By following the Macedonia2025 example of engagement and partnership, people who want to champion their home countries can willingly step up to take on the challenges and partner with others to find and implement solutions.

SHRI STUDIO & SERVICE CORPS: SUPPORT, HONOR, RESPECT, INSPIRE

In our final story of this chapter, we turn to the United States—and the smallest, but most densely populated state in the country, Rhode Island, where a big impact is being made by someone who is truly one of those guys: Alison Bologna. An award-winning local television news anchor, yoga enthusiast, and advocate for the underserved, Alison is a force of nature. Through Shri, with its headquarters in Pawtucket, Alison offers low-cost and free yoga classes in a 15,000-square-foot historic building that she bought and revitalized. In addition, Shri's outreach brings yoga programs to other locations, such as schools, shelters, residential treatment centers, senior centers, and hospitals. Shri serves a wide population, including adults and children with intellectual and developmental disabilities, veterans and active military personnel, incarcerated youth, people in recovery, children in hospitals and shelters, senior citizens, and others.

"Why is it that most often white women with disposable income are the ones with access to yoga?" Alison remarked. This rhetorical question highlighted the Shri mission: serving a variety of people who usually are not able to practice yoga.

Yoga is known to offer numerous therapeutic benefits: preventing or reducing physical and emotional pain; helping reduce stress, anxiety, and depression; improving strength and flexibility; enhancing respiratory and cardio-vascular functions; and supporting recovery from addiction.[6] While Alison believes strongly in yoga's impact on a person's overall health and well-being, she does not preach. She simply reaches out to organizations across the community with the invitation to bring in people to try a class.

Shri serves more than 8,500 students a year. Of that total, 4,000 students and their partner agencies are offered free classes through Shri's nonprofit arm. On any given day, more than 100 students participate in Shri classes, and there are more than 40 instructors who teach off the "Shri curriculum" that Alison wrote.

This is the essence of *karma yoga*, as Alison called it. "It's better to act than not to act, and the goal is to not have an attachment to the outcomes." Alison (who also teaches classes) and other Shri-certified teachers show up each day because they have the skills and experience that can benefit others. Fundraising and grants ensure the teachers are paid, while students with special needs receive the appropriate classes for free. Even members of the public who take classes at Shri pay far less than they would in comparable studios.

I asked Alison to go back to the beginning to answer the question: why yoga and why Rhode Island. Her answers reveal a path of purpose and finding a sense of home.

Born in Connecticut, Alison spent much of her youth in Southern California, where her father ran biotechnology companies. As an undergraduate, she went to Northwestern University's Medill School of Journalism, graduating in 1997, and then earned a graduate degree at Columbia University. She was hired immediately as a producer for NBC's *Dateline* in New York City, but after four years wanted to pursue on-air reporting. When an opportunity arose at the local NBC affiliate in Rhode Island, Alison decided to give it a try. "When I moved to Rhode Island, I had no family or friends here. But I remember feeling this sense of home," she said. "I got here and dug in."

The Shri Yoga values on display.
Source: Courtesy of Alison Bologa, Shri Yoga.

In 2010, Alison made a significant change in her life. While continuing as an award-winning news anchor (with a stint in Boston), she opened her first yoga studio in downtown Pawtucket, an economically depressed industrial city in Rhode Island. Alison had been practicing yoga since her days in New York City to reduce stress and to support a healthy lifestyle, and she wanted to bring that experience to her home community. She chose the name *Shri* because of its multiple meanings. One is that it derives from the Sanskrit word loosely defined as light, radiance, and abundance. It is also an acronym for the organization's values that came to Alison one day: "Support, honor, respect, inspire." Now those words are displayed everywhere—on the walls of the studio and on the t-shirts worn by Alison and other staff. These values are also introduced at the start and end of every Shri class.

Over the next decade, Shri grew beyond the capacity of three leased spaces. That's when Alison decided it was time to find a permanent home for the studio. Pawtucket Mayor Donald Grebein suggested she look at an old mill that was on the National Register of Historic Places and a short walk to a new commuter rail hub. In Alison's eyes, the site was perfect, albeit in need of significant renovations.

Alison finalized the purchase of the property in January 2020, only to have her redevelopment plans sidelined by both the COVID-19 pandemic and a massive fire at an adjacent property. Construction costs skyrocketed over the next two years, and the project exceeded its original budget by more than $700,000. Through each challenge, however, Alison remained resolute, a defining trait we have seen throughout this chapter and among others who commit to a vision and mission. Zoning changes and access to grants and other state funding incentives helped move the project forward, and in late August 2023, Alison officially opened the mixed-use, mixed-income building that is now home to Shri and other wrap-around services for the community, including an art center and a food pantry on the first floor. Upstairs, Alison designed eight apartments (five of which are deed-restricted affordable units) that provide quality housing for adults with intellectual and developmental disabilities who can access any of the services in the building. The first tenant to move into an affordable housing unit was a 62-year-old man with an intellectual disability who comes downstairs four days a week for free yoga classes that are appropriate for him. The final phase on the campus includes the renovation of a blighted, one-story garage in the parking lot that is being repurposed into a cafe for a workforce development and employment program for disabled adults.

From Pawtucket, Shri extends its inclusive yoga outreach model into the community to offer yoga at multiple locations including but not limited to Bradley Pediatric Hospital, a local psychiatric hospital for children, in addition to the state's psychiatric hospital; the local Veterans' Administration facility; an Alzheimer's disease day program; shelters and schools. Free programs are funded by a variety of sponsors and foundations, such as CVS Health, Blue Cross & Blue Shield of Rhode Island, and private foundations. In addition, Shri has a retail end: selling whole-grain, nut-free Shri Bark snack bars, rounds and muffins (created by Alison's husband, an Emmy Award–winning news photographer in Boston who also loves to cook) to help fund the free yoga classes. Among Shri Bark customers are public schools for their free and reduced-cost breakfast and lunch programs.

Currently, Shri serves Rhode Island, parts of northern Connecticut, and southern Massachusetts, with hopes of expanding throughout New England. Everywhere Alison looks, she sees so many schools where physical education teachers and social workers are eager to offer classes to help students with fitness as well as social and emotional health—and far more hospitals, clinics, and other facilities that support people with addictions, eating disorders, and others in recovery. It's one of the blessings and challenges—the community of people to help gets larger, not smaller.

To serve these broader needs—and to do so with in-person classes that provide the full yoga experience—Alison is exploring licensing the curriculum and training more outreach students to become paid Shri teachers for their peers.

"This is the larger strategy of putting skills into action," Alison said. "I am all about consistency."

With that one word, Alison evoked a key principle I talk about in my leadership classes and presentations: as I tell my students and executives alike, the only way to get things done is with discipline, focus, consistency, and credibility. It's showing up for others—not just one time, but over time. This is what creates a legacy.

"That's very important to me," Alison added. "I don't want this to disappear when I'm gone."

BECOMING ONE OF THOSE GUYS

From local communities to entire countries, there is a need for more people who not only see problems but also look for and implement solutions. Rather than wait to see who will show up to make a difference, we need to remember—*we are those guys!*

With gratitude for what we have, appreciation for those who have helped us, and a willingness to share with others, we can make a difference in the lives of all people—whether in our community, across our country, or around the world. It is living the Golden Rule: treating others the way we want to be treated, with respect, dignity, and care.

With an open heart, a curious mind, and a generous spirit, we engage in some self-reflection as we ask ourselves these questions:

- *What problems or challenges capture our attention— intellectually and emotionally?*
- *What skills, talents, and experiences do we have that could help others?*
- *Where in our community (local or global) do we feel drawn to make a difference?*
- *What organization or individuals do we know who are doing something similar?*
- *And finally—the most important question of all: what's holding us back?*

PART THREE

CREATING OUR FUTURE

Just as we were influenced by those who came before us, we strive to become role models for those who follow us. Often, this happens within families, but there is also another intergenerational aspect. We seek to identify and develop leaders who are closest to the problems and challenges.

This is how legacy lives on.

CHAPTER 7

A GLOBAL
FOOTPRINT

*"Let us not be satisfied with just giving money. Money is not enough . . .
they need your hearts to love them."*

—*Mother Teresa*

When Andrew Youn graduated from Kellogg in 2006, he
could have easily pursued a career in the for-profit
world. Any investment bank or consulting firm would have
gladly hired him. Instead, Andrew took an entirely different
path. He pursued his passion for helping farm families in
sub-Saharan Africa through an organization he cofounded:
One Acre Fund.

Readers of my previous books are familiar with One Acre
Fund, which today serves more than 4 million farmers in
Kenya, Rwanda, Burundi, Malawi, Uganda, Ethiopia, Zambia,
Tanzania, and Nigeria. Now, in this book, I am once again
featuring Andrew's story because, in my opinion, it is the
most powerful example I know of building a legacy from
scratch and having a truly global impact. Let's put it this way:
20 years ago, One Acre Fund did not exist. Today, One Acre

145

Fund has set a goal that, by 2030, it will serve 10 million farmers and, in doing that, serve 10% of the families in the world living on less than $1 per person, per day.

This help is coming at a crucial time. Climate change and rising temperatures are a worldwide problem. In sub-Saharan Africa, the projection is for severe droughts and cyclones that are both more frequent and more intense. The ravages of weather threaten food supplies for millions of people. According to scientists, rising temperatures in developing countries will significantly affect agricultural output, increasing the risk of hunger and famine. Rising temperatures and greater variability in rainfall will contribute to shorter growing seasons and shrinkage of arable land. The land that remains for farming could be at risk of being overused, making it less productive.[1] Of all those affected, smallholder farmers who support themselves on plots of land that are often no more than one acre—and many times far less—are likely to feel the worst of it.

As a nonprofit social enterprise, One Acre Fund provides smallholder farmers with seed, fertilizer, training, and better access to the marketplace. It works with farmers directly by delivering what it calls "a bundle of farm services,"[2] and indirectly through partner organizations to further extend its reach.

The legacy of One Acre Fund is measured not only in the number of smallholder farmers who have access to the means to earn their way out of poverty but also in the development of a new generation of leaders. Through a decentralized leadership model, One Acre Fund is identifying, training, and developing leaders in the sub-Saharan countries where it operates. We will meet one of those leaders, Pauline Wanjala, later in this chapter.

Over the years, I have had the pleasure of getting to know Andrew, who has maintained close ties to Kellogg. Several of his Kellogg classmates were among his earliest financial supporters, and each year Kellogg students, faculty, and alumni donate to this very worthy organization. Andrew's inspiring example is felt on the Kellogg campus in other ways, as well. The Youn Impact Scholars, endowed by a gift from Christopher and Courtney Combe in 2013, are Kellogg students and alumni who are passionately committed to social impact. Starting with the first cohort in 2014, each year a new group of Youn Impact Scholars is named in recognition of their commitment to change and receive support.

I am a proud supporter of One Acre Fund, donating all my proceeds from book sales and my speaking fees when I give talks, presentations, and seminars on values-based leadership to organizations around the world. I am grateful that my legacy as a values-based leader can help support the legacy being built by One Acre Fund. But it's not enough to just send money. I wanted to see the work of One Acre Fund in action and to share the experience with my wife, Julie, and our children. So, in 2016, my family traveled to Kenya to visit the farms where One Acre Fund brings help and hope. We saw firsthand that One Acre Fund's work is not a handout, but rather a hand up by empowering farmers through training and low-cost loans.

And it all began with a young man who wanted to change the world.

ANDREW YOUN: A HEART TO SERVE

Like many people profiled in this book, Andrew credits his family as being role models for serving others. His parents emigrated from South Korea to the United States and soon became involved in community service. In middle school and high school, Andrew tutored students who came from disadvantaged backgrounds. In college, he worked in a food pantry—though perhaps not in the optimal way, Andrew admitted. "I thought I could make the pantry more effective by making them a database. It wasn't a harmful thing, but also not really helpful." Looking back, we can see the germ of an important lesson that Andrew would later learn in Africa: the help you *think* others need may not be what they really need.

After college, Andrew volunteered at a homeless shelter, which directly influenced his choice of summer internships while he was at Kellogg. He helped hundreds of patients enroll in a South African AIDS treatment program—and, for the first time, felt that he was able to make a difference at a meaningful scale. After working all summer in South Africa, Andrew took what he called a "random trip" to Kenya. Little did he know at the time this trip would be the start of a life-changing journey.

While in Kenya, Andrew met two farmers who were neighbors. One struggled to provide for her family and had lost a child to the effects of poverty and hunger. The other farmer, though, was able to produce four times as much food on the same size parcel of land. When Andrew asked the second farmer what she was doing differently, she described how she was using naturally grown seed and microdoses of fertilizer.

"Those two farmers inspired what became One Acre Fund," Andrew recalled. "How could we help the farmer who struggled to be more successful like her neighbor?"

During his second year at Kellogg, Andrew hired some-one on the ground in Kenya to operate a pilot project with 40 farm families, funded with $7,000 of his own savings. "It worked," Andrew said. "But I was also incredibly naive—I had no idea what I was doing. Those farmers, though, had outstanding harvests. It speaks to the power and simplicity of the program."

It's important to understand that Andrew did not come from a farming family, nor did he have a background in agri-culture. He was an economics undergraduate from Yale, pursuing an MBA from Kellogg. These facts, alone, could have convinced Andrew that he really couldn't help the farmers in Africa. He could have left it to someone else—the multinational nongovernmental organizations that address poverty and hunger as part of their missions—to do all the work, while he got a job, made a lot of money, and sent in donations occasionally.

But that's not how Andrew is wired. Being on the ground in Kenya, he was convinced that someone had to do something—and he couldn't wait for someone else to step up to help. He had to try. Andrew referred to this attitude as "start where you are and just do it."

Andrew was so eager to begin his venture, he skipped the Kellogg graduation and immediately moved to rural Kenya. To earn their trust and build rapport, he lived with the peo-ple. He invested months learning from them and ensuring the farmers he met that "we're not here for the short term."

When Andrew talks about working closely with farmers, this isn't just rhetoric. He left the United States in 2006 and lived in East Africa for 18 years, mostly in rural areas. When it comes to having a global impact—leaving behind a foot-print on the world—Andrew and his colleagues are all-in.

From the beginning, the One Acre Fund mission has been to help local farmers increase their crop yields to feed their families. This priority addresses what might seem like an oxymoron: a hungry farmer. In fact, it might strike us as unfathomable that someone who grows crops can experience hunger and witness their children becoming sick and dying. It's not just because of crop failure due to drought and climate change. The problem is that farmers in Africa typically have very small plots of land that make it difficult to yield a big enough harvest to feed a family.

The result is what's known around the world as the *hunger season*—the time between when the food from the last harvest runs out and a new crop is planted. As the UN's World Food Program USA explained, "Also known as the lean season, the hunger season brings with it difficult choices. Fathers find odd jobs to buy food at high prices . . .; mothers try to stretch whatever food they can scrounge to make it last; or families leave their home altogether to find food. Children eat a less varied diet, becoming more vulnerable to sickness and malnutrition. Death rates spike for those children worse off."[3]

Only by learning to grow more on their land can farmers produce enough to feed their families and sell the surplus to purchase supplies and send their children to school. One Acre Fund also increasingly assists farmers with handling and marketing their produce to earn higher prices for their work.

But not everything One Acre Fund has tried, especially in the beginning, has worked out. In fact, like any new organization, it has had to endure its share of failures. Among the early failures were attempts to (in Andrew's words) "impose too many of my own beliefs onto our farmers." This included growing fancy, high-valued crops that we might associate with organic farming in the United States—passionfruit, mushrooms, and other highly perishable export crops. But there wasn't much demand for tons of chili peppers in rural Kenya.

From early failures, One Acre Fund learned the lesson of listening intently to its customers. The smallholder farmers know what they need—and do not need. This is the same approach taken by Kheyti to develop a low-cost greenhouse by listening to the smallholder farmers it serves in India (as profiled in Chapter 4). One Acre Fund not only pays close attention to what farmers are experiencing and saying, but Andrew and his colleagues also see them as "our bosses."

This attitude established One Acre's mantra of "Farmers First." As Andrew said, "It is constantly learning and seeking to serve in a better way. We get a lot of feedback from farmers—and that has led us to new areas."

A One Acre Fund farmer, in her field.
Source: Courtesy of One Acre Fund.

For example, over the years of working with farmers, One Acre Fund has heard their complaints about not having enough wood for cooking fires. With the land becoming deforested, farmers must spend more and more time gathering firewood. In response, One Acre Fund started a tree-planting program that, to date, has planted 150 million trees. In 2022, alone, it supported the planting of 62.8 million trees, with more than half (56%) surviving the first year. Seedlings can die due to heat stress, animal grazing, and pests—risks that One Acre Fund hopes to mitigate through more farmer training. Its goal is to plant a total of *1 billion* trees by 2030. Given the impact of climate change around the planet, and the need for reforestation in sub-Saharan Africa, tree planting will become another part of One Acre Fund's lasting legacy.

Farm families also need better sources of light and heat within their small houses. The typical household in rural Africa relies on burning kerosene in tin cans. This not only consumes costly fuel but also emits unhealthy fumes indoors. As research has shown, kerosene lamps used indoors can increase the risk of diseases such as tuberculosis and acute respiratory infections in children, as well as safety hazards such as burns.[4]

The UN Sustainable Development Goals (SDGs) highlight a variety of urgent needs around the globe and especially in developing countries. Among them are poverty reduction, improved health (particularly for women and young children), clean water, education, gender equality, and access to economic opportunity. One specific goal—SDG 7—seeks to "ensure access to affordable, reliable, sustainable, and modern energy for all."[5] Can One Acre Fund, which seemingly has its hands full with training and helping farmers to grow more crops, really take on sustainable energy? It can and it did by stepping up to help farm families with indoor lighting sourced by solar power. To date, One Acre Fund has financed and made available to farmers more than 2 million solar lanterns.

Changing the World—With Partners

Every time I speak with Andrew, I am both inspired and energized. Maybe it's my background as a CFO, but I love hearing "the numbers." Crop yields, on average, grow by about 40%. The lives of more than 10 million children have been positively affected. One of my favorite statistics of all is One Acre Fund's goal of reaching *20 million children* in farm families.

As inspiring as that number may be, it takes a pragmatic approach. One Acre Fund cannot reach that many children alone. Instead, it is partnering with others—including the Kenyan and Rwandan governments—to extend One Acre's reach and benefit the lives of many more farm families and children across the region.

In the 18 years since One Acre was founded, the organization has amassed a rich legacy of lessons learned. Top of Andrew's list is the power of partnership. For example, by working with the government of Rwanda, One Acre Fund can tap into its network of 14,000 farmer trainers who reach every village in that country. "We support our government partners in any way they need," Andrew said. To help farmer trainers, One Acre Fund designed picture-based training materials that break down language and literacy barriers.

"What's really powerful is, it's not about us. It's about this amazing effort by the Rwandan government to serve their people. We want to be in service of that," Andrew said. "It's a reminder that we're more powerful when we travel together."

A relatively new partner for One Acre Fund is a Kenyan seed company that is interested in expanding to Rwanda. One Acre Fund has worked for years with many seed companies to procure supplies for farmers, such as maize, sorghum, millet, bean, and collard seeds. The Kenyan seed company, however, faced risks in entering a new market. Believing that having access to another supplier would ultimately benefit the farmers, One Acre stepped in to help facilitate the Kenyan seed company's venture by sharing the financial risk.

What's even more interesting is how interconnected One Acre Fund's partnerships have become. In this example, the Rwandan government grows the seed, the Kenyan company provides technical resources and assistance, and One Acre Fund distributes the seed to hundreds of thousands of Rwandan farmers. "That could triple by the end of the decade," Andrew said. "That's an important aspect of partnership to us."

Partnerships also remind us of the benefit of engaging as many different groups as possible. To have a global footprint, an organization cannot go it alone. By joining forces with others, fractured efforts are combined and aligned. Experiences are shared, and information is disseminated broadly. Unfortunately, among some nonprofits working locally and globally there is an unfortunate tendency to carve out their "turf." They put stakes in the ground around "this is where and how we work," and compete rather than collaborate. As a result, despite good intentions and a lot of hard work, there is no economy of scale. Projects end up siloed, and the same mistakes are repeated by others, over and over. But it doesn't have to be that way.

"Through partnerships, we can all dream bigger," Andrew said. "And the bigger we get, the more responsibility we take on. That compels us to reach out to more partners, to further extend our reach."

A Legacy of Local Leaders

One Acre Fund has intentionally tried to listen to the people it serves—for example by locating its largest headquarters in rural areas. As discussed previously, the farmers who are closest to the problem often have insights into potential solutions. Second, the organization relies on a decentralized leadership structure that helps ensure decision-making is as close as possible to One Acre Fund's clients.

At the top is One Acre Fund's global leadership council that sets organization-wide strategic goals and vision. Its 18-person council has more than 50% representation by women and/or nationals of African countries. At the next level are country directors and deputy country directors. Together, this group sets long-term operational and expansion goals for their teams, guides financial strategies, and provides input about country staffing and projects. Then there are field staff management teams and 23 senior field directors who lead field operations. Field leaders manage large teams and ensure that farmers receive the products and training they need. At the field level, these leaders hold One Acre Fund accountable for providing quality, valuable services that improve farmers' abilities to feed their families and increase their incomes. Today, One Acre Fund employes nearly 8,300 people, largely in rural areas.

PAULINE WANJALA: FROM LOCAL FARMER TO SENIOR LEADER

One Acre Fund also identifies those with leadership talent within the local communities it serves. Among the farmers there are those who have innate talent and a desire to learn more skills. An inspiring example is Pauline Wanjala. Now a senior leader in the Upper Western Region of Kenya, Pauline first learned about One Acre Fund as a farmer, growing beans on a small plot in Kenya.

When I spoke with Pauline, she told the story of her journey with One Acre Fund, beginning in 2008 when she first heard about farmers in her village learning to improve their practices for growing beans. At the time, Pauline was part of a group of five farmers, led by her grandmother. Each week, her grandmother attended One Acre Fund training and then brought the information back to the other farmers.

"We were like pioneers, learning new things," Pauline said. "Instead of scattering the seeds, we were given training on how to plant beans in rows. We could see that each seed gets enough fertilizer without wasting it. We took the time to focus on every seed and weeded in a timely manner." In addition, instead of planting maize and beans together, the farmers were taught the importance of allowing each crop to grow separately, so as not to compete for nutrients, water, and sunlight.

Because of her grandmother's age, however, it became difficult for her to attend every training session. Pauline volunteered to help with her grandmother's duties, then eventually took her place as the group leader. "As I was taught, I carried the same information back to the group," she explained. "I would visit the other farmers' fields. If there were any challenges, I could tell them what I learned."

These farmers had very small plots of land, some as little as an eighth of an acre. Pauline's grandmother had one of the larger parcels, measuring a quarter-acre. On these small pieces of land, farmers had to grow enough to feed their families. Every year it was a struggle.

The harvest of 2008, however, was a different story. Pauline, her grandmother, and the other farmers in their group could not believe their eyes. Their yield was 300% more than their previous harvests. "My grandmother was the happiest woman," Pauline remembered. "When the neighbors saw it, they kept asking us, 'How did we do it?'" When the answer was what they'd learned from One Acre Fund, more farmers began to enroll in the program.

During this time, Pauline completed her university education, where she studied horticulture. Her background and experience helping other farmers made her a perfect candidate to become a field officer for One Acre Fund. She joined in September 2008, just a few months after she had received farmer training from a field officer.

To take on her first professional role with One Acre Fund, Pauline received training in a variety of areas: client relations, public speaking, time management, and leadership skills. The more she learned about farming practices and techniques, the better Pauline could help others improve their harvests. She was especially interested in helping older farmers who, in addition to training, often needed help implementing new practices in the field.

As a field officer, Pauline had 11 clients. To support them, she received training from a field manager. But after only two weeks on the job, Pauline was called in for a meeting. "As I traveled to the office, I was doubting myself. What did I do wrong? Then, when I got there, I saw the field manager who had been training me. I hadn't seen him in the field for several days," Pauline said.

By the end of that meeting, Pauline was promoted to field manager. The person who had previously held that position was reassigned as a field officer. Instantly, Pauline recognized the importance of supporting her former supervisor who had, in essence, been demoted. "I told him that it does not matter what positions we are in. We both have to make sure we are supporting the community," Pauline said.

By 2009, Pauline's responsibilities increased as One Acre Fund expanded from helping farmers grow beans to cultivating maize. "So that meant helping more farmers and getting more people out into the community," she said. In this position, she was overseeing five field officers, servicing a total of 308 clients. It was her responsibility to ensure they had the information and support they needed to train farmers in growing multiple crops. As a first-time field manager, Pauline kept the group aligned by reminding them of their mission: "We are looking to create a positive impact in our community," she said. "The farmers are the central people we are looking at. We want to make sure they have a smile on their faces."

When the harvest came in, those smiles broadened. The abundance showed the positive impact of the training and support in the field from One Acre Fund. That, in turn, led even more farmers to join.

In 2011, Pauline was promoted again, becoming a senior field manager who oversaw the field managers in her district. "It was leading leaders," she recalled. "It was ensuring that the field managers could mentor, support, and build up the field officers in their district."

Then, in 2012, Pauline was asked to become field director of the Lugari District, located in Kenya's Western Province. By 2013, the Lugari District had grown from 23 sites to 42 sites, with each site serving more than 300 clients. One Acre is about empowerment and access to affordable supplies and services, including low-cost loans—not charity. When local farmers value the assistance and guidance they receive, and reap the benefit with bigger harvests, they can repay their small loans and generate revenue that goes to helping others.

Enrolling farmers in this model takes training to get their buy-in, and Pauline recalled proudly how the Lugari District had the most success in terms of farmer retention and repayment of loans in all of Kenya. In fact, in 2013, 100% of the loans made to farmers in Lugari District were repaid—a track record that any bank in the United States would envy!

At the start of 2014, Pauline was summoned to the One Acre Fund office. "Again, I asked myself, 'What did I do?'" she said. "That's when I was told, 'You are being promoted to senior field director, to be in charge of other field directors.'"

Then in 2016, she became a project specialist and, in early 2020, was promoted yet again to senior project specialist. In 2021, she became manager of the Upper Western Region, which includes several districts. Remarkably, in just 13 years, Pauline advanced from a volunteer in her village who farmed only a third of an acre to overseeing One Acre Fund activities in a large section of Kenya. And she wasn't done yet. In 2023, Pauline was made regional manager, overseeing both One Acre Fund's services to farmers in the field and the retail side of bringing the harvest to market.

Along her career journey, Pauline has had to balance all aspects of her life—being a mother, a wife, and an employee, all of which demand a share of her time and attention. There have been times she needed to step back, self-reflect, and find a way forward. She strives to find a way to "give my work uninterrupted attention during the stipulated hours so that I can wind down with my family in the evening. I have learned to take a break and defer any work that eats into my family time. In case of any urgent work matters, I am comfortable having earlier mornings to complete unfinished business and meet my deadlines."[6]

Pauline has found a way to pursue balance (I don't think any of us ever really achieve it). In fact, I think she could teach my MBA students a thing or two about being centered in purpose, being clear about goals and priorities, and finding a way to make the most of what I call *your 168*—the number of hours in a week that we are all given.

Defining Success by What Others Achieve

At the end of Pauline's story, I was a little breathless. She had moved up so far and so fast within an organization that is highly professional and serious about leadership development. No matter how many different responsibilities and bigger roles Pauline took on, I was impressed by how her commitment never changed: "seeing our clients be successful."

I was also struck by how Pauline exemplifies values-based leadership. As I've said countless times over the years, leadership is the ability to influence others. Values-based leadership takes it to the next level. By their word, action, and example, values-based leaders seek to inspire and motivate, using their influence to pursue what matters most. For Pauline, what matters most is the mission of One Acre Fund: "Farmers First!" Or, as she explained years ago to the field managers who reported to her at the time, "I don't want us to look at who is this and who is that—their title and role. Our focus is on ensuring that everything we do is helping our clients—that after joining One Acre Fund, our clients see a positive impact."

Of all the farmers she has worked with, one in particular continues to stand out in Pauline's mind: a woman she met back in 2008 after becoming a field officer. At the time, this woman lived in a grass hut with her children, and she struggled to grow enough food to feed and support them. After learning about One Acre Fund, the woman decided to take on a small loan to obtain the seed and fertilizer she needed and committed to learning better farming techniques. "Because of her hard work, she was able to repay everything," Pauline said excitedly. "Now I see her living in a permanent house. I called her to say, 'I am happy for you.'"

Even more inspiring than what this woman achieved were her words to describe what she experienced. "She told me, 'Nothing is impossible.' Now, when I look at her, I can see that we can change the lives of so many," Pauline said. "We see them prospering and succeeding."

A Global Footprint

On the organizational level, One Acre Fund is expanding the good that it does across sub-Saharan Africa. Theirs is a model that has proven to be scalable *and* successful to train, mentor, and empower farmers who are the solution to poverty and hunger everywhere, and especially in sub-Saharan Africa. The impact is generational: grandparents, parents, and children—and those who will follow. The children who grew up in farm families helped by One Acre Fund are now beginning to farm themselves, becoming a second generation of clients.

Like every organization, One Acre Fund is composed of individuals—people who willingly take on the problems they see around them and provide solutions. That includes people like Pauline. She was not only given multiple opportunities to advance, but she seized each one with purpose and intention. From a local field officer to running a large district, Pauline remains committed to farmers who need to learn how to grow their way out of hunger and poverty.

When I told Pauline, "You're literally changing the world," she laughed a little out of modesty. Then she quickly pivoted to the person who had started her on this path: her grandmother, who died several years ago. People in her home village still recall this older woman—this matriarch within the group of farmers—who gave them hope and determination to learn new ways of growing their crops.

In the same way, her grandmother's example continues to inspire Pauline. "We can climb the mountains together," she said. "We can change the lives of other people."

FROM A TINY SEED

What is the difference between hunger and having enough? For the farmers of One Acre Fund, it comes down to a sack of seeds, some fertilizer, and training in farming techniques. Over and over, from one farm to the next—across communities, districts, and regions—the benefits spread. With one good harvest, the dreaded hunger season becomes a bad memory of a former time.

And it all came from a chance encounter nearly two decades ago, when Andrew Youn met two farmers in Kenya. From that tiny seed of an idea, a thriving social enterprise has grown and continues to spread across Africa. It's an inspiring example of what can happen when one person decides that making a difference is possible.

Inspiration is also a call to action. Our world has no shortage of crises to address and urgent problems to be solved. For some, taking action will likely mean making a donation to support the legacy of individuals and organizations doing the good work. There's certainly nothing wrong with that.

But for a few people—perhaps one or two readers of this book—seeing how One Acre Fund is leaving a global footprint might help germinate the seed of their own ideas. Or, as I like to describe it, they don't just want to watch the movie—they want to be in the movie!

So I leave you with a question for your self-reflection:

■ *What will you do to answer the call?*

CHAPTER 8

THE CYCLE
CONTINUES

"Those having torches will pass them on to the others."

—*Plato*

What does it mean to create a legacy that will last well beyond our own lifetime? In contemplating this question, many people will probably focus on their family, encouraging the next generation to get involved in volunteering and other charitable activities. Others may think in fiduciary terms, of setting up an endowment or trust. And some may gravitate toward a larger picture to help a cause gain traction across a broader community, including young people who will take up the mantle of leadership and advocacy.

All these answers address different aspects of creating a legacy that outlives us by engaging future generations. This might bring to mind the work of famous philanthropists. Nineteenth-century industrialist Andrew Carnegie founded the Carnegie Foundation, which has taken up causes in education for more than a century. John D. Rockefeller Sr. and his son, John D. Jr., established the Rockefeller Foundation,

165

which today engages in philanthropic work around the globe. However, a lasting legacy can also be created with a simple step: sharing the experience of giving to others with one's children and grandchildren.

Good works and charitable actions can be the common ground that links past, present, and future. Here, we go full circle from the discussion in Chapter 1, of recalling our own early influences—often parents and grandparents—who taught us the importance of caring for and giving to others. Now, in that same spirit of giving, we intentionally engage those who will come after us.

In this chapter, we feature the stories of people who established a legacy in their lifetimes and are now involving the next generation. This passing of the torch makes legacy a gift of living a values-based life, as well as a responsibility to perpetuate those values. With so many issues and needs in our world, and so much polarity that continues to divide people, building a multigenerational legacy helps bring healing and cohesion to our communities.

One example is a family foundation. As the name implies, these foundations are established by a family who sets aside a portion of their wealth as the seed capital for making donations and offering grants to charitable causes for many years to come. Family members run the foundation and decide where donations should be made. Over time, the foundation and its works pass from one generation to the next.

In this chapter, two family foundations are profiled—not for their size, but for what they represent: the desire of a family to work together to do good in the world. In keeping with the stories told thus far in the book, one foundation is focused locally and the other globally.

PACIFIC SPIRIT FOUNDATION: BREAKING
DOWN BARRIERS IN THE COMMUNITY

This story begins about a decade ago, when Gottfried "Guff" Muench retired as president of both Cummins Western Canada, a distributor for Cummins, which makes engines and generators, and Cummins Westport, an alternative fuel technology company. As he thought about a vision for his life over the next three decades, he contemplated the example of his mother. A Yugoslavian refugee of modest means, she always tried to make a better life for her children. Following in her footsteps, Guff and his wife, Beverley, had already done that for their two sons. But what about contributing to a better life for other people's children—especially youth who encountered barriers in the community? "We had worked hard, and we were fortunate. Things had gone well for us," Guff told me. "We wanted to give something back to society."

In looking at the kind of legacy he wanted to establish, Guff also drew on his long career with Cummins and the influence of a long-time leader, Irwin Miller, who had risen from general manager to become chairman and CEO. He not only set a strategic direction for the company but also founded the Cummins Engine Foundation in 1957 and later paid the fees for talented young architects to design public buildings to enhance the quality of life and culture in Columbus, Indiana, where the company is headquartered.[1] Guff experienced the Cummins corporate legacy of philanthropy firsthand when he and his family lived in Columbus and were expected to "show up and volunteer" in the community.

Drawing on all these experiences and influences, Guff and Beverley decided to establish a family foundation to do good works in their home community of Vancouver, British Columbia. The result was the Pacific Spirit Foundation.

For Beverley, who was born in Newfoundland and then later moved to Canada's western provinces, establishing a foundation resonated with earlier life experiences of giving back to others. In addition, Beverley had a long career in technology, working for companies such as GTE and IBM, which enabled her to help fund the foundation. Guff and Beverley donated some of their stock holdings in Cummins and IBM when the foundation was established. Today, that initial funding has grown to more than CAN$13 million, of which the foundation spends 3% annually or nearly CAN$400,000 a year. "That will be in perpetuity, for our children, grandchildren, and great-grandchildren to manage," Guff said.

With money to invest, the question then became how. As the saying goes, the only thing harder than making money is knowing where to spend it.

Working with a consultant, Beverley began to draft a mission statement for the foundation. Soon, it became a family project, involving Guff and Beverley, and their sons, Peter and David. The mission captured a vision and an action plan: "to enable disadvantaged youth within Vancouver, especially Downtown Eastside, to create lives for themselves which were previously not an option due to circumstances beyond their control."

Although Vancouver is one of the wealthiest cities in North America, very little of that prosperity or potential is visible in Downtown Eastside. One of Vancouver's oldest neighborhoods, Downtown Eastside and its residents face complex problems, including crime, drug use, unemployment, homelessness and other housing issues, and a loss of businesses in that community.[2]

Peter Muench, Guff and Beverley's oldest son and a former Kellogg student in my MBA class, recalled his dad purposefully driving him through Downtown Eastside on their way to see a hockey game. "These kids on the street in Downtown Eastside were roughly my age or younger," Peter recalled. "My dad wanted me to see them—to pay attention to people who could so easily slip through the cracks. I could see how just a couple of things could knock you off your life trajectory and set a different outcome."

That realization had a powerful impact on Peter as a youth, and it has stayed with him now that he's an adult, married, and with a young child.

From Small Giving to Bigger Projects

In the beginning, Pacific Spirit Foundation engaged in what Beverley called "exploratory funding" across several groups committed to helping disadvantaged youth in Vancouver, and specifically in Downtown Eastside. "We did a gazillion little things, but found that was hard to manage," Beverley said. More recently, Pacific Spirit has undertaken two large projects in the community.

The first was helping to fund the Firehall No. 5 project, partnering with the YWCA, the City of Vancouver, and the Canadian government to provide housing for single mothers and their children—most after suffering domestic abuse and other trauma. The four floors above the firehall have been refurbished into two- and three-bedroom units of low-cost housing, along with a rooftop patio. A second project is the expansion of Covenant House in Vancouver, which provides housing and developmental resources to at-risk youth and those in crisis. The people it serves face a variety of urgent risks and dangers: human trafficking, mental health issues, bullying, and other crises that can lead to homelessness. By providing a safe place to stay, Covenant House supports young people in their transition to healthier, independent futures.

The common denominator of these two projects is the concept of home. To explain, Beverley cited a quote attributed to the Dalai Lama: "Home is where you feel at home and are treated well." That feeling, however, has been largely absent in the lives of at-risk youth in Downtown Eastside. "When kids don't find a champion at home to help them, they end up on the street," Beverley added. Firehall No. 5 and Covenant House, however, are striving to provide a welcoming place for young people who long to feel safe and need to learn how to advocate for themselves.

Through the Firehall No. 5 and Covenant House projects, Pacific Spirit focused on building walls—the physical structures that house and protect people. Now the foundation's focus is shifting to building programs. "It's not creating something new. Rather, it's finding someone who is already doing something and partnering with them to ramp it up. We want to help leverage programs that can really help youth," Guff said.

For Guff, especially, prevention is a major emphasis, such as intervening with youth who are at risk of dropping out of school and heading to the street. "We want to get to that 15-year-old before they're on the street and using drugs, before they're involved in crime," he added. "It's being proactive, not just reactive."

From One Generation to the Next

As the founders of Pacific Spirit, Guff and Beverley are turning increasingly to their sons, Peter and David, for what the foundation will look like as its mission evolves and it partners with new organizations. It's a leadership responsibility they've been groomed for from the beginning.

"Our parents used the foundation as an education for David and me," Peter said. Given that background it's not surprising that Peter and his wife, Amber, have had "a lot of talks about our values," starting from their earliest days of dating. "A lot of our relationship has been built around morals and ethics that were compatible."

Although their daughter, Elaine, is only one year old, Peter looks forward to her growing up with awareness of the foundation and how it unites the family in giving back to their community. "It will be a wonderful lesson to share with Elaine—that there is a moral obligation to give back to the world in some way," Peter said. "That's particularly important if life has dealt you a good hand."

THE GALLAGHER FOUNDATION: IN THE FOOTSTEPS OF THEIR FATHER

"It's not about me." With those words, my good friend J. P. Gallagher started our conversation with a disclaimer. "This is about my father and my family."

I had reached out to J. P. because of our long-standing connection. J. P. is the CEO of Endeavor Health (formerly NorthShore University Health System), where I have been a board member since 1997, including two terms as board chairman. In writing about the Gallagher Foundation for this chapter, I reached out first to J. P.

Founded by J. P.'s father, the late Jerry Gallagher, and his mother, Ellen, the Gallagher Foundation builds leadership capabilities in developing countries by providing scholarships to high-potential students in need of economic and other support. The foundation has been active in South Africa, Mexico, and Turkey—carrying out Jerry's vision, which is very much supported by Ellen. Today, the foundation is truly a family affair.

A Chance Encounter on a Golf Course

The story begins with Jerry Gallagher, who was born in 1941 in Easton, Pennsylvania. His family lived modestly, and Jerry realized from a young age that any opportunities he wanted to pursue, he would have to create for himself. He enrolled in Princeton University on a Navy ROTC scholarship and graduated with an aeronautical engineering degree in 1963. To fulfill his military service obligation, he served as an officer aboard US Navy submarines from 1963 to 1967. After discharge, he pursued a business degree, receiving a full scholarship from the University of Chicago, where he earned his MBA in 1969.

Jerry Gallagher: 1941–2014.
Source: Courtesy of the Gallagher Family.

The takeaways from Jerry's young life are twofold: first, his drive and ambition that underscored a strong work ethic and, second, the value he placed on education.

In 1970—coincidentally, the year J. P. was born—Jerry went to Wall Street, working at Donaldson, Lufkin & Jenrette, becoming the firm's retail industry analyst and receiving recognition, including the "All American" designation from *Institutional Investor*. Jerry also created a performance metric for retail companies known as "same store sales growth" to provide an apples-to-apples comparison of performance, which is still used today.

In 1976, Jerry moved to Minnesota to join retailer Dayton-Hudson (which later became Target), became chief financial officer of its Mervyn's operation on the West Coast, and then went back to Minnesota to assume the role of vice chairman. Then, in 1984, Jerry returned to the investment world, working for a boutique firm for the next 27 years, where he sponsored investments in 38 retail companies—household names such as Dick's Sporting Goods, Office Depot, PetSmart, P. F. Chang's China Bistro, Potbelly Sandwich Works, Ulta Salon Cosmetics & Fragrance, and Whole Foods.

As Jerry's career grew, so did his financial success, to a level that exceeded his expectations. Like Guff and Beverley Muench with their Pacific Spirit Foundation, Jerry and Ellen Gallagher wanted to show their appreciation by giving back to others. The question was how.

Yes, they could make donations and support local and global causes, but they wanted to do more to make a lasting difference in someone's life—and through them to help a larger community. That's when a chance meeting on a trip to South Africa planted a seed for what became the Gallagher Foundation.

In 2000, Jerry and Ellen traveled to South Africa to visit friends. While there, Jerry and his South African friend played golf on two different days. Their caddy the first day was a young man in his early 20s, whom they later learned was from the Zulu tribe. On the second day, the caddy was back. Jerry later learned that the young man had come to the golf course two hours ahead of time to make sure he got to caddy for him again. At the end of the second round, Jerry noticed that the caddy signed his name with an "X." That's when Jerry realized that this bright young man was illiterate because he'd never had access to education. Here was a reminder of the repugnant apartheid policies and racial discrimination that had been institutionalized in South Africa, from European colonization through the early 1990s.

Meeting this young man made an impression on Jerry, and he resolved to do something to help correct the systemic imbalance created by racist and segregationist policies. Back home in Minnesota, Jerry and Ellen brainstormed what they should do—and, in 2001, the Gallagher Foundation was born. The mission was to provide full college scholarships for young future leaders with economic need so they could receive an education and reach their full potential.

Given Jerry's initial inspiration it made sense for the newly formed Gallagher Foundation to begin its work in 2002 in South Africa, with an inaugural class of five scholars to attend the University of Cape Town. A leading university, it had a history of opposing apartheid, especially in higher education. The university first admitted black students in the 1920s, and a small enrollment continued over the years. Later in the

20th century, the number of black students admitted greatly increased. By the time the Gallagher Foundation sent its first scholars to the university, half the student body was black. (In honor of the caddy who had inspired this work, for many years the foundation made sure that one of the South African scholars selected was from the Zulu tribe.)

The foundation paid the students' full tuition, room and board, expenses to attend social events, and even provided money for them to go home to visit their families. As J. P. explained, "It's one thing to pay for college, but you can't drop off these students and say, 'Go figure this out.' We pay for them to get together, to go on field trips, to socialize, and then to help each other. It's a community of Gallagher Scholars. And a big part of that community is navigating through college." In this way, the scholars are supported academically and emotionally.

For the Gallagher family—Jerry and Ellen, and their three children, Ann, J. P., and Megan—the foundation quickly became a focal point. For Megan, the foundation would become her vocation.

Growing and Going Global

Like the rest of the Gallagher children, Megan Gallagher Prindiville was supportive of her parents' endeavors with the foundation, but she never saw it as being part of her life plan. She had a degree in special education and moved to Seattle, where she taught for four years as she and her husband saved for an adventure they'd been planning. They bought a VW van and drove around the United States and Canada, visiting national parks and doing volunteer work, such as for Habitat for Humanity. By the end of the trip, they decided where they would live: Minneapolis.

Megan had planned to return to teaching, but now that she was pregnant, it did not make sense to her to start a job and then take maternity leave. That's when Jerry approached her with an offer to help with the foundation, which at the time was in its second year of operation. Megan agreed and began working about 10 hours a week. A year and a half later, Jerry approached Megan again. Although very supportive of Megan going back to teaching, he laid out what was next for the foundation. The more she listened to her father's plan, the more intrigued Megan became. When Megan agreed to stay on, they were both excited about the potential to grow the foundation and its activities together.

Megan was expected to treat it like any other professional position and build her skills, such as taking accounting classes and honing her business acumen. "Dad was a businessman, and from the beginning he was adamant about running a nonprofit efficiently, like a business," she added. "At the time, a well-functioning nonprofit was about 70% of funds going to a specific need and 30% for overhead. Dad wanted to get to 90% and 10%, to make sure we were spending money as effectively as possible."

To expand beyond South Africa, Jerry and Megan created criteria for selecting the next country. After looking at several possibilities in Latin America, the foundation decided to expand to Mexico. In 2004, the first class of Gallagher Scholars in Mexico were enrolled in what is now Tecnológico de Monterrey. A year later, Jerry wanted to add a third country to the scholarship map—and preferably a predominantly Muslim country. That led to the selection of Turkey and the first class of scholars from that country to attend Boğaziçi University.

Across these three countries, a diverse group of scholars represented a broad range of ethnic, cultural, and religious groups. What they all had in common, though, was a commitment to become professionals and leaders who could contribute to the economic development of their home country. Truly, it was a future-focused legacy that would extend even beyond these individuals, to the people they would one day hire, manage, develop, and mentor.

The Torch Is Passed

From her initial position of director of administration, Megan became vice president of the foundation, but was still working part-time. Then, in 2014, Jerry Gallagher died suddenly from a brain aneurism at the age of 73. At the time of his death, the foundation had sponsored more than 150 Gallagher Scholars in South Africa, Mexico, and Turkey.

One of those scholars—a young woman from South Africa—came to his funeral. She was in the United States at the time, getting a graduate degree from Stanford. (Three of the Gallagher Scholar graduates have been offered full scholarships to Stanford's MBA Seed program.)

"When she gave her remarks at the funeral, the entire church was in tears," J. P. said. "The foundation was still fairly new at this point. We said to ourselves, whatever we do, we have to make sure it continues."

As the person who had worked day-to-day with their father on the foundation, Megan faced a major decision of whether to take over running it full-time. "I had a really good conversation with my family. J. P. was really supportive—he told me, 'We'll find the right person to run it if you want to do something else or if you don't want to go full-time,'" she recalled.

Her children were older, and she had both the passion for the foundation and the capacity to take on a bigger role. "I can remember thinking that we can't hand this over to someone else. It [the foundation] wouldn't be sustainable," Megan said.

Although the foundation was funded in perpetuity, from an organizational perspective, "we were not there yet" in terms of sustainability, Megan explained. As the new president of the foundation, she was the only full-time employee. The foundation had country directors, but no other processes and systems in place.

Jerry and Ellen had been scheduled to go to South Africa in August 2014. It was the kind of trip Jerry made every year to interview new candidates and meet with current and graduated scholars. His death in July meant the trip had to be postponed a month, but in September Megan and her mother, Ellen, went to South Africa. The foundation funded scholarships in all three countries that year, continuing its work without interruption.

In addition to Megan as president, the next generation stepped up in governance, as well. Serving on the foundation board, in addition to Ellen as cofounder, are the other two Gallagher children and all three spouses: Ann and her husband, Brad Diemer; J. P. and his wife, Krista; and Megan's husband, Matt Prindiville. J. P. has served as chairman of the foundation board for nearly 10 years.

More changes were coming that would further expand the activities of the foundation, beyond the family. A year after Jerry's death, Megan invited two former Gallagher Scholars (or Gallagher Graduate Scholars, as the foundation calls them) to join her on the interview panel in South Africa. "In that moment, I thought, 'This is happening! This is the dream.'"

It had been Jerry's vision all along to involve the graduates as part of the sustainability of the foundation. "Dad had said, 'One day, we'll have graduated scholars sitting next to me in interviews—when they have enough experience.' That is one nugget he had given me before he passed," Megan explained.

The Gallagher Foundation strives to forge strong connections among scholars and alums to build a community. For example, leadership summits are held annually within each country, with graduates helping to build the curricula. Typically, these sessions are organized on a particular leadership trait—for example, what it means to be an ethical leader.

Megan recalled the first time a graduate panel was convened in South Africa, eight years ago. Scholars were invited to ask anything, and graduates gave honest, real-world answers. "I'll never forget it," she recalled. "The graduates talked about what it's like being the only Black person in the boardroom or the pressure of having to give financially to their families, while also building themselves financially."

Flash-forward to 2022—the 20th anniversary of the foundation. The three country programs, while very successful, remained segmented as three distinct communities. Megan wanted to change that with the establishment of a robust global alumni network. She proposed to the board a global leadership summit, suggesting that it could be a "changemaker" for the foundation. The board agreed, and the Gallagher Foundation's first Global Leadership Summit was convened in Vienna, Austria, in September 2023. The event brought together 146 people, spanning nine countries, who came together for three days. Among them were scholars and graduates from South Africa, Mexico, and Turkey.

A highlight of the program was a leadership session led by Zipho Sikhakhane, a 2005 alum of the program. After graduating from the University of Cape Town, she attended Stanford Business School, and now owns a South Africa–based global consulting firm. It was a full circle moment: a promising student who had been chosen 18 years earlier to receive a scholarship now giving back as a leadership summit speaker, teaching others.

"It exceeded my expectation—a truly phenomenal event. Every table had people from every country. We worked incredibly hard to mix the group—and to offer a balance between leadership curriculum and social events," Megan said. "On Saturday night, in a beautiful place in Vienna, we brought everyone together."

The Gallagher Foundation hosts its first annual Global Leadership Summit in Vienna. Ellen Gallagher, cofounder, stands in the middle of the front row.
Source: Courtesy of the Gallagher Foundation.

At the end of the evening, Megan made an impromptu announcement: "Let's dance." Two hundred people were suddenly on the dance floor. Then something magical happened. The Turkish, South African, and Mexican scholars not only performed traditional dances from their cultures, but also taught them to each other.

That moment became an epiphany for Megan: "I really saw the cultural importance of our mission. Yes, part of what our organization is all about is helping these countries through the scholars. At the same time, their cultures are very important to them. Seeing that expressed on the dance floor was one thing I didn't even try to plan."

The next day, on the first flight of her return trip, Megan spent two and a half hours jotting down notes. When she got home, she called J. P. and excitedly told him, "I know what the future of the foundation could be," and then laid out the three phases she was envisioning.

The first phase encompasses the current work of the foundation to develop scholars. The second phase would begin two years before the scholars graduate and extend through two years after graduation—focused on how to help them be successful. "More than just getting that first job, it's how we support them in that job," Megan said.

The third phase is summed up in one word: *networking*. This would leverage the global reach of more than 20 years of scholars of various ages and stages of professional development. As of this writing, the Gallagher Foundation has about 55 active scholars who are currently undergraduates, as well as more than 200 alums who are members of the community and serve their countries in various professions. For example, one Gallagher Graduate Scholar is currently the head of international trade for the South African government. Another is a former professional soccer player who got his degree in Mexico, went to work for McKinsey, and now plans to return to Mexico to help young entrepreneurs. This is an invaluable alumni network, steeped in leadership values.

"We have been explicit about keeping the alums connected—hoping they will feel a sense of paying it forward to help others," J. P. added.

It is inevitable that global changes, particularly political ones, will affect the program. In 2023, the foundation announced that, due to "changes in the political structure" in Turkey (where the government has become more authoritarian and reportedly has targeted critics and dissidents),[3] it will no longer provide any new scholarships in that country. It was a difficult, emotionally painful decision. However, the foundation emphasized that current scholars and alums will continue to be supported.

Megan is currently leading the foundation through a very deliberate process to select the next countries to be added to the Gallagher Scholars program. She has enlisted the help of an international firm to look at a variety of factors and indices that correlate with developing young talent in developing countries. In time, the foundation will extend its reach once again.

The Next Generation

As the Gallagher Foundation looks to the future, it is also emphasizing succession planning for leadership and governance. In the short term, there will be opportunities to involve the next generation of family members, such as introducing them to the work of the foundation as well as the scholars in the program.

"When we travel, we look for ways to connect with scholars—especially having our children meet and talk with them," J. P. said. "We're trying to cultivate a sense of family—that when they accept the scholarships, they are joining our family."

As the next generation of Gallaghers matures, some will no doubt find their roles—perhaps meeting candidates and helping to interview prospective scholars. In the years ahead, they may join the board. But involving the next generation doesn't mean only the Gallagher family.

Megan and the foundation board are committed to offering more programs and connections for the Gallagher Scholars and alums. For example, each country has a Graduate Advisory Council that meets four times a year on projects that support scholars, graduates, and the community. In addition, two or three graduates serve on the panels interviewing prospective scholars, along with Megan and the country director. Other opportunities for the graduates include assisting with recruiting, reviewing applications, mentoring scholars, and hosting and/or speaking at gatherings.

"We have this network and it's growing. Some of our graduates are 40 years old now—they have been in their professions for years. It's more than just 'come back and see everybody' or 'come hang out at a barbecue.' Rather, there's more opportunity to develop this network," Megan said.

One day, a Gallagher Graduate Scholar could serve on the foundation board. It is a very real possibility as the foundation expands and matures. "I am optimistic that the foundation board will look very different than our family over the years," Megan said.

This is a meaningful and inspiring way to bring in the next generation, beyond family members. Exemplary leaders who graduate from the scholar program—who have unique experiences and perspectives that relate not only to their own country but also to the developing world at large—are an asset to the organization. Including these voices in programming, leadership, and governance will ensure the foundation remains strong and serves its mission for many more years to come.

LEARNING WHAT THEY LIVE

It's a poem that most of us (particularly those who are parents) have seen or read—in the pediatrician's office, in a school building, or in the room where Sunday school classes are taught: "Children Learn What They Live" by Dorothy Law Nolte. It goes like this: "If children live with criticism, they learn to condemn. If children live with hostility, they learn to fight . . ." It then concludes with an inspiring vision: "If children live with security, they learn to have faith in themselves and others. If children live with friendliness, they learn the world is a nice place in which to live."[4]

What appear to be simple, inspiring words are also a call to action. One generation has a responsibility to provide the life experiences that will shape the next. As parents and grandparents, as aunts and uncles, we have a crucial role to play—and not just by our words. It's our actions that the next generation will notice.

This is the real meaning of building a legacy, from one generation to the next. It doesn't require the wealth or complexity of a foundation. A lasting legacy can be built by getting the family together to sponsor or participate in a community project. Ideally this isn't "one and done," but an ongoing commitment by two or more generations to create shared memories and lessons learned. There is no shortage of possibilities, such as food drives and neighborhood cleanups.

Beyond the good works to be done, there is another reason to build a legacy across the generations. Our children and grandchildren will learn by what they live.

And so, we reflect:

- *What causes and concerns speak to us—and are we literally speaking about them to our families?*
- *What values do we want to convey to our children and grandchildren—and how are we doing that?*
- *What actions can we take together—bringing together the generations—in our communities?*
- *What kind of world do we want to leave for those who will come after us?*

CHAPTER 9

WHAT THE WORLD NEEDS NOW

"There is always light. Only if we are brave enough to see it. There is always light. Only if we are brave enough to be it."
—Amanda Gorman

It's a sad, irrefutable truth: our world today is polarized to the point of being fractured—along political lines, economic divides, and widening inequalities. The International Monetary Fund described it in clear and blunt terms: "Global inequalities are in bad shape and mostly do not appear to be getting better. Disparities today are about the same as they were in the early 20th century."[1] In the United States, with the approach of the presidential election in November 2024, the political divide is deepening, and people are described as more disillusioned with politics now than they have been in decades. The Pew Research Center's American Trends Panel, in attempting to capture the political environment in just one word, came up with a disheartening list: "Disgusting, divisive, dysfunctional. Corrupt, crazy, confusing. Broken, bad, sad."[2] Without making any political commentary about one side or the other, we see that brokenness is the status quo.

And yet, that is not the whole story.

In researching this book and listening to the stories of people building lasting legacies, other words emerged. *Pay it back. Pay it forward. Help others. Make a difference. Purpose. A calling.*

These phrases are echoed on every page of this book. Among so many people, there is a deep and genuine desire to do something—locally or globally—to improve the world, or at least our corner of it. Reflecting on this commonality leads to a conclusion about what the world needs now, perhaps more than at any other time in history: hope.

Hope reminds us that change is possible, that out of darkness can come light. We just need to believe and then take action to make it so—for ourselves and future generations.

NATURE AND NURTURE

Some may see my hopeful view as optimistic at best and naive at worst. And yet, I think hope is inextinguishable. Viktor Frankl called it "faith in the future," as he described what kept him and fellow prisoners alive during their internment in Nazi concentration camps. As he wrote in *Man's Search for Meaning,* "The prisoner who had lost faith in the future—his future—was doomed. With his loss of belief in the future, he also lost his spiritual hold; he let himself decline and became subject to mental and physical decay."[3] If through the bleakest times in our human history—famines, war, persecution, countless natural disasters—people found reasons to keep hope alive, why should we stop now?

There always have been and, I am confident, always will be those who step up to serve others. One theory is based on altruism being part of our biological nature. A fascinating article described altruistic behavior even among animals, particularly species that live within complex social structures. It's called *biological altruism,* and examples include vampire bats that feed other members of their group to keep them from starving (involving the regurgitation of blood, which I'd rather not think about). Among many bird species, a nesting pair get help in raising their young from "helper birds" that protect the nest and assist in feeding the fledglings. Certain kinds of monkeys alert others when a predator is near, even though their cries of alarm will attract the attention of the predator and potentially put themselves in danger. Even insects can be altruistic, such as worker bees that spend their lives caring for the queen bee, building the nest, gathering food, and tending to the larvae—the next generation of bees.[4] At the risk of oversimplifying what is undoubtedly very complex, I find it enlightening and comforting to reflect on creatures giving of themselves without any personal benefit. They do so, even without conscious thought. Perhaps it really is in our nature to give.

As the stories shared in this book show, altruism is also grounded in our "nurture"—the values we learned from our families and other positive influences, such as our culture, community, and faith traditions.

For me, practicing my faith takes many different forms. This includes going to church services, reading scripture, praying regularly (at least once a day), and attending an annual three-day retreat (as described in Chapter 2). My faith also provides a lens through which I view every aspect of my life, including why and how I give to others.

I'm not in the business of forcing my beliefs on anyone. The interesting thing, though, is that when I do reveal the importance of faith and spirituality in my life, it forges a connection with other people. No matter how different our practices and perspectives—even when I'm talking with someone who is agnostic or atheist—as we frame our discussion around living a values-based life, there is much common ground. For example, in my classes we discuss the importance of self-reflection (as we did in this book, in Chapter 2)—tuning out the noise and engaging in self-examination for 15 minutes a day. Afterwards, I often receive questions from students that go even deeper. Some people will share how they practiced a faith tradition when they were younger, but stopped in high school, and now wonder if it's time to reexamine that part of their lives. Others don't practice a religion, but consider themselves somewhat spiritual, and want to talk about taking self-reflection to the next level.

My daily practice of self-reflection is tied directly to my faith. In contemplating my values, my sense of purpose, and what matters most in my life, I continuously step back and consider the bigger picture. As my grandfather taught me so many years ago, we're only here for a short while—the blink of an eye. This is an invaluable perspective that focuses my attention on what I do and how I act. It's not all about me!

Far more than success any of us might enjoy is a sense of significance—of having done something that matters. This only comes from making a positive difference in the world and being a force for good. Every day, I strive to use the gifts God has given me to make things better for others. Personally, I believe it's what we are all called to do—especially in today's world, which is in such need of hope and healing.

This confirmation of purpose has been the unexpected gift of writing this book. At the outset, I expected more of a discussion about the importance of values-based leadership in establishing and building a legacy for the future. I pictured a few stories to illustrate the key points. But the deeper I engaged in the writing, the more I saw that the stories themselves were what people needed to hear. Each one holds immeasurable inspiration and motivation of how to act with selflessness, compassion, and generosity.

So many people are building bridges across communities and borders. Within my personal network is someone who leads an advocacy group for immigrants, particularly those who are undocumented and face the daily risk of incarceration and deportation. At a time when immigration is cited as the biggest political issue on the national agenda, this group and the person in my network intentionally keep a low profile. They don't publicize what they do, so as not to draw unwelcome attention. Nonetheless, they bravely engage in advocacy by raising their voices for legislative changes in immigration, visiting immigrants and offering direct assistance, and praying for those at risk of deportation. In one recent communique, the group provided a long list of names of people currently jailed by US Immigration and Customs Enforcement. "The great majority are likely to face deportation within the next few months, resulting in separation from family and/or friends," the group stated. After deportation, they will "return to a country in which many have not lived for years."

Whenever I hear about this work on behalf of those who have no political voice and few (if any) advocates to help them, I recall the Bible verse: "For I was hungry and you gave me something to eat, I was thirsty and you gave me something to drink, I was a stranger and you invited me in, I needed clothes and you clothed me, I was sick and you looked after me, I was in prison and you came to visit me" (Matthew 25:35–37). If we need a model of altruism, here it is, in these ancient and enduring words.

FROM THE POPE TO POP MUSIC

Although my religious life informs the legacy I strive to build, it is not the only place to find inspiration. We can find role models and examples in so many areas—including some unexpected ones, such as rock 'n' roll.

I love music. When it comes to having fun, it's in the top three in my life. When I was CEO of Baxter, I often had meetings every hour throughout the day. But occasionally, an opening would suddenly appear in my schedule—such as when my assistant, Kathy, would tell me a meeting was canceled because of flight delays. I knew exactly what to do: I grabbed my car keys, drove to a McDonald's nearby, got a Diet Coke at the drive-thru, and sat in the back of the parking lot with Bruce Springsteen tunes cranked up full blast. Forty-five minutes later, I was back in the office, relaxed and refreshed. Now that you know this about me, you'll understand why I have found inspiration among the biggest stars in music.

An example is Bono, lead singer of U2, who is famous for such rock anthems as "Beautiful Day," "Bloody Sunday," and "With or Without You"—among so many others. He has also taken to the world stage for humanitarian efforts, such as poverty, the global AIDS crisis, and injustice. For years, I have admired Bono's willingness to use his celebrity and influence to put the spotlight on global issues. The nonprofit he cofounded, ONE, seeks to end global poverty especially among women and girls by urging governments to increase their aid to the underprivileged. He also cofounded Rise Fund, a global impact fund investing in entrepreneurial companies focused on social and environmental change in support of the United Nations' Sustainable Development Goals.

Bono has received numerous prizes and accolades for his humanitarian work. He's been *Time* magazine's Person of the Year and has been honored by the French and British governments, as well as the City of Dublin. In addition, he has forged a kind of kinship with two leaders of the Roman Catholic Church. In 1999, he met with Pope John Paul II to discuss the plight of poor nations around the globe. Bono reportedly dubbed Pope John Paul II as "the first funky pontiff" after he picked up a pair of the performer's signature wraparound sunglasses and put them on.[5]

In 2022, in a private audience at the Vatican, Bono extolled the importance of girls' education as "a superpower in fighting extreme poverty," and asked Pope Francis for his thoughts on women and girls playing a "powerful role in tackling the climate crisis." Pope Francis replied: "We always speak of Mother Earth and not Father Earth"—prompting reporters to declare Bono and Pope Francis to be "in harmony," even without singing.[6]

I share this story because it illustrates how caring for others and our planet brings together people from diverse backgrounds and perspectives. We don't need to be "singing the same tune"; we can each march to a different drummer, to paraphrase Henry David Thoreau. And when our voices do come together for a common cause, something miraculous can happen.

"WE ARE THE WORLD"

One of the most memorable songs of 1985 was "We Are the World," featuring more than 40 top performers—Dionne Warwick, Diana Ross, Bob Dylan, Michael Jackson, Cyndi Lauper, Paul Simon, Willie Nelson, my favorite Bruce Springsteen, and many others. The song was recorded in one long night on January 28, 1985, to raise money for famine relief in Ethiopia, where more than a million people had died of starvation.

Like most people of my generation, I knew the song and could sing at least the chorus: "We are the world. We are the children . . ." Then, as I was writing this book, a friend of mine insisted that I watch a new documentary (released in January 2024) entitled *The Greatest Night in Pop*. I watched and listened, with a smile on my face and often tears in my eyes, as the documentary retold the story of that one epic night when, against all odds and seemingly insurmountable logistical problems, some of the most successful and in-demand performers came together to record a song that would leverage their talent and name recognition into a hit single to raise money for others. No one made a dime on the project—not the performers, the sound engineers, or the film crew who captured the original footage. All proceeds went to famine relief.

The inspiration for "We Are the World" came from a British-Irish collaboration of pop artists calling themselves "Band Aid," who in 1984 recorded "Do They Know It's Christmas" to raise money for famine relief in Ethiopia. This led the late artist and activist Harry Belafonte to observe that American artists, particularly black stars of the industry, needed to step up. As Lionel Richie, the organizer, coauthor of "We Are the World," and a featured performer, quoted Belafonte as saying to him, "We have white folks saving black folks. We don't have black folks saving black folks. We need to save our own people from hunger."[7]

Lionel Richie said yes—and so did so many others. Tempers flared and egos got a little bruised at times, as the documentary candidly shows. But these superstars came together in what can only be called a glorious celebration of humanity. (Don't take my word for it: see the film on Netflix or, at least, the highlights on YouTube.) At the end, one of the last people to leave the recording studio was Diana Ross, the legendary lead singer of The Supremes who had gone on to become a solo superstar. When asked why she was still there, Diana said tearfully that she didn't want it to end.

I knew exactly how she felt, as the credits rolled, I didn't want the documentary to be over. In fact, I immediately watched *The Greatest Night in Pop* a second time—and not for the last time.

This is also how I feel as this book comes to its last chapter. I don't want it to end. I want to keep reaching out across the country and around the globe to unearth more stories of people who are not only trying but also succeeding in making a better life for others—and a better world for all.

FOLLOWING THE LIGHT OF THE LUMINARIES

Now, in these last pages, I want to capture a few more inspiring examples, especially those that, like "We Are the World," highlight people who use their names and their fame to do good in the world. Contrary to what we often associate with celebrity culture—trendsetting that is steeped in consumerism—this is where we can find compelling examples of humanitarianism.

Luminaries who lend their light to others can be found in every field—sports, arts, and entertainment. The causes they champion are just as varied, from illiteracy in rural America to the global refugee crisis. At a time when celebrities continue to dominate both traditional and digital media, we can find among them some compelling examples of what it means to do good with what you have been given. Following is a sampling of people I admire for their talent and their charitable work.

Walter and Connie Payton Foundation

Among Chicagoans who remember the glory days of the Chicago Bears (the 1985 Da Bears!), football legend Walter Payton remains a household name. His talent was evident from his earliest days. A player at Jackson State University, Payton was on the starting lineup his freshman year in 1971 and went on to be selected for the All-American team and was named Black College Player of the Year in 1973 and 1974. Payton joined the Chicago Bears in 1975 and was chosen for the Pro Bowl nine times. Toward the end of his 13-year career with the Bears, he helped bring a Super Bowl victory to Chicago.

It wasn't just his talent as a football player that attracted attention. Payton, nicknamed *Sweetness,* was also known for helping others. In 1998, Payton raised his many charitable activities to another level with the Walter Payton Foundation, dedicated to supporting the neediest children in the United States. Then, in early 1999, Payton announced he had a condition known as sclerosing cholangitis—blockage of the bile ducts. A few months later, he died of bile duct cancer. His type of rare cancer, stemming from a chronic illness, raised awareness of the need for organ donations. Soon after his death, in fact, the Chicago-area organ donation office was overwhelmed by responses. In 2007, the Walter Payton Liver Center opened at the University of Illinois, offering medical and surgical treatment from a world-class team of physicians and surgeons using the latest technology.

Payton's foundation has been renamed the Walter and Connie Payton Foundation, to recognize the ongoing efforts of his wife to carry out the legacy of helping children and veterans. And every year, Connie helps choose the "Walter Payton NFL Man of the Year" from players nominated by their teams for their contribution to the community.

"They have been given a blessing and they are really willing to bless other people because truly that's how Walter and I lived our lives," Connie told Chicago's Channel 2 news. "We were blessed."[8]

Her words remind me, once again, of my favorite saying from the Gospel of Luke: where much is given, much is expected.

The Dollywood Foundation

Born and raised in Pittman Center, a town in Sevier County, Tennessee, Dolly Rebecca Parton was the fourth of 12 children in her family. She began performing at the age of 10, made her debut at the Grand Ole Opry at age 13, and moved to Nashville to launch her music career the day after she finished high school in 1964. Today, she is a superstar in music, television, movies, and her namesake theme park, Dollywood.

Dolly Parton also exemplifies a values-based leadership principle I call *genuine humility*—best described as never forgetting where you come from. This can be seen in her Dollywood Foundation, established in 1988, to support children in Sevier County, Tennessee, to pursue educational success. For example, in the early 1990s, Dolly promised $500 to every seventh and eighth grader who graduated from high school; as a result, the dropout rate from these two classes was reduced dramatically, from 35% to 6%. In addition, the Dollywood Foundation offers five scholarships to the county's high school seniors to help pay for education at any accredited university, as well as additional scholarships.

In 1995, the foundation launched a monthly book giving program for children under age five through Dolly Parton's Imagination Library in Sevier County. What began locally became an international movement in partnerships with other organizations that adopt the program. To date, more than 230 million books have been donated.

Her inspiration, Parton has said, was her father who was illiterate because of a lack of access to education. "Like so many country people, the hard-working people, especially back in the rural areas, my dad never had a chance to go to school because he had to help make a living for the family. And so, Daddy couldn't read and write," she said. Thinking of his example and imagining what her father might have accomplished with an education led Parton to "do something that would inspire kids to love reading and to love learning."[9]

Through the legacy Dolly has built, the inspiration of her hard-working father fights illiteracy and lifts others out of poverty and into opportunity.

Angelina Jolie: United Nations High Commissioner for Refugees

She is an Academy Award–winning actress with instant name recognition for her movies as well as the Hollywood "news" that has made her face familiar to all. But Angelina Jolie has also established a far more impactful legacy: spending more than 20 years serving the United Nations High Commissioner for Refugees (UNHCR—the UN agency that serves refugees). For more than two decades as a Goodwill Ambassador, Jolie traveled to countries around the globe to meet with refugee communities and to advocate for refugee families and asylum seekers.

Even a glance at the UNHCR website pages dedicated to Jolie and her missions reveals an impressive track record. She is not a celebrity commenting on world events from afar. She has been on the ground as a special envoy to places such as Jordan, Iraq, Lebanon, Ecuador, Peru, Bangladesh, Kenya, and Colombia. As she stated in 2021, on a visit to the Goudoubo Camp for refugees in Burkina Faso, "I have seen the conditions inflicted upon refugees globally—the hunger and suffering and insecurity and lack of aid, let alone justice—because we pick and choose which conflicts to pay attention to and for how long; because governments turn a blind eye to abuses when it is convenient; and because we as individual citizens feel powerless to change that."[10]

Although her UN service has ended, Jolie continues humanitarian work in places like Cambodia, a country she first visited while filming her movie *Lara Croft: Tomb Raider*. While on set in Cambodia, she adopted her first child, Maddox Jolie-Pitt, and later established a foundation that bears his name. Today, the activities of the Maddox Jolie-Pitt Foundation include environmental protection and clearing landmines. In addition, the foundation focuses on access to food, health, and education in Cambodia, where nearly 20% of the population lives below the poverty line.[11]

Listening to a BBC interview with Jolie, from nearly a decade ago, I was struck by her candor and openness as she related a visit to Sierra Leone, which at the time was torn by violence. "My whole life changed. I realized how sheltered I'd been and how fortunate I was."[12] With these words, this movie star brought a new twist on the words I often say about getting involved: "We don't just want to be watching the movie; we want to be in the movie."

Jackie Chan: UNICEF Ambassador

With dazzling martial arts skills, actor Jackie Chan has starred in numerous movies that combine his signature moves with the timing of a comedic actor. His is a "rags-to-riches" story in Hollywood, making a name for himself by performing his own stunts, then later earning millions of dollars per picture. He is also known for movies with a moral message, such as fighting for the underdog and delivering a good story without sex or graphic violence.[13]

In 1988, his Jackie Chan Charitable Foundation was formed to support numerous philanthropic organizations globally. In 2004, Chan was named a UNICEF Goodwill Ambassador, advocating for children—especially those who live in poverty, have HIV/AIDS, or are survivors of landmine injuries. As of this writing, he remains involved with UNICEF.

In a simple statement after his appointment to UNICEF, Chan articulated his mission. "Let me know whatever I can do, wherever I can go. I promise you I'll do it."[14] If ever there was an anthem for building a legacy, that is it.

FOLLOWING THE LIGHT OF OTHERS

It's important to remember that it doesn't take a million-dollar smile for the camera (or millions to give away) to make an impact. We can extrapolate from the examples of these luminaries in bringing light to our own communities. For example, those who are drawn to Angelina Jolie's work with refugees can look for programs in their own communities. One place to investigate is a local faith organization that may sponsor or participate in a refugee program. The Minnesota Council of Churches has been active in helping resettle refugees, most of whom are from Burma, Somalia, Ethiopia, the Democratic Republic of Congo, and Ukraine. As the council states, "Refugees want to participate fully in life without the fear of violence or persecution. With a little help when they arrive, refugees become contributing Minnesotans. Welcoming refugees is in line with our Minnesota values."[15] Or, if Dolly Parton's work on literacy and education touches our hearts, there are any number of ways to carry out similar work in our own communities, from volunteering at the local library or with a program such as Head Start, which offers early childhood education in local communities.

Being inspired by others is only the start; it's what we do with that inspiration that makes a difference.

OUR BUTTERFLY EFFECT

It's a quotation said in various ways, attributed to numerous sources, and with several interpretations. "When a butterfly flaps its wings in (name location), it can cause a tornado (or a typhoon) in (name other location)." However we say it, there is a butterfly effect in building a legacy. The good we do today can have a positive and long-lasting impact locally and perhaps even globally. All it takes is showing up and doing what you can, the best that you can.

Where do you begin? Right where you are. We return to the practice of self-reflection to help you focus on what you see, hear, sense, and feel in this moment. Ask yourself, "What is the difference I want to see in the world?" The more you go inward, the better you can focus outward to see where and how you can make a difference in the lives of others.

As I see it, no matter our religious or spiritual background or philosophy on life, most of us long to feel connected to something larger than ourselves. For some, that may be a sense of purpose or a mission; for others, it is serving God. Whatever terminology we are most comfortable with, living and leaving a legacy will take us on a path that often becomes a spiritual quest.

For me, nothing captures the spiritual core of a values-based life and building a values-based legacy than "The Peace Prayer" attributed to St. Francis of Assisi. In my mind, the opening lines of this prayer transcend any belief system, tradition, or philosophy:

> *Lord, make me an instrument of Thy peace;*
> *Where there is hatred, let me sow love;*
> *Where there is injury, pardon;*
> *Where there is error, the truth;*
> *Where there is doubt, the faith;*
> *Where there is despair, hope;*
> *Where there is darkness, light*
> *And where there is sadness, joy . . .* [16]

FINAL THOUGHTS

No matter how long or short our time here on earth, we all are allotted the same number of hours each day, and each week contains the same number of hours for everyone—168, my favorite number! The only variable is what we do with those hours.

If you believe that you should devote some of those hours to making a difference and leaving a legacy, all you need to do is open your mind and your heart to the possibilities. There is much to do, in big ways and small. No effort is immaterial or unimportant. But it does take a first step to start a lifelong journey.

Everything you do to help make a positive impact goes far beyond your own effort. Just as you were inspired by the people who shared their stories in this book, your example may inspire someone else. Then they, in turn, can motivate someone else. It's a multiplier effect of good and grace. By what you say and do, the commitments you make and the convictions you hold, your desire to live a values-based life will become a values-based legacy—and one will that last far beyond your lifetime!

EPILOGUE: MY INSPIRATION

It is quiet in my house. Everyone is asleep—except me and my grandson, Harrison, who just stirred and needed to be rocked. Holding him in my arms, I am transported back to when I was a father for the first time, and Julie and I took turns walking the floor with our firstborn, Suzie. Now, I'm cradling Suzie's son.

My grandson, Harrison Thomas Clark.
Source: Courtesy of the Kraemer family.

Harrison's eyes are wide open, fighting sleep. As we settle into my rocking chair, I hope the sound of my voice soothes him—or, at least, we keep each other company during this late hour.

The manuscript pages of this book are on my desk, and so I read aloud from them. Suddenly, I'm choked up. This grandchild in my arms epitomizes for me what it means to build a legacy—and leave to others. Just as my grandfathers, Farrell Grehan and Harry Kraemer Sr., influenced me, so I hope to do the same for Harrison (and other grandchildren who may bless our family one day). And not just them, but every child, everywhere around this world.

The next generation is one of the main reasons we strive to do good in the world, making it better in tangible ways. The world they are inheriting is so different from what we knew growing up: a climate crisis; deeper social, economic, and political divides; and the crushing impact of poverty, hunger, and injustice. But we are leaving them something else, as I have tried to capture in this book: a legacy of hope.

As long as there is a desire to do good for others, the world is not a lost cause. It can be renewed and restored. For Harrison and the 2 billion children around the world under the age of 14, we say, thank you for bringing out the best in us.

ACKNOWLEDGMENTS

First and foremost, I want to thank Tricia Crisafulli and Patrick Commins for their tremendous work in making this book a reality. Tricia played a key role in the development of my first three books, and this fourth book has the added advantage of including the work of her son and business partner, Pat.

I also want to acknowledge the many individuals who took the time to meet with me and share their stories. I am honored to feature their legacies in these pages.

Thanks also to those who took the time to read numerous drafts of the book and provided valuable insights and input: Dr. Daven Morrison; my daughter Shannon; my sister, Marilyn Foreman; my cousin Christopher Grehan, who researched and provided family photos; and my friend Ben Zastawny.

And, in everything I do, my special thanks to my life partner of almost 50 years, Julie Jansen Kraemer, who somehow has the patience to put up with my crazy schedule and late-night phone calls that made this book possible. Life with you and our five children—Suzie, Andrew, Shannon, Diane, and Daniel—and our new son-in-law Casey and daughter-in-law Katelyn is truly a legacy I cherish.

ABOUT THE AUTHOR

Harry M. Jansen Kraemer Jr. is an author of four values-based leadership books: *From Values to Action: The Four Principles of Values-Based Leadership, Becoming the Best: Build a World-Class Organization Through Values-Based Leadership, Your 168: Finding Purpose and Satisfaction in a Values-Based Life,* and his latest, this book: *Your Values-Based Legacy: Making a Difference at Every Age and Phase of Life.*

A clinical professor of leadership at Northwestern University's Kellogg School of Management, Harry has been named Kellogg School Professor of the Year for the full-time program as well as for the executive MBA programs in Chicago, Miami, and Hong Kong. He is also an executive partner with Madison Dearborn Partners, a private equity firm based in Chicago. Previously, he had a 23-year career at Baxter International Inc., a $12 billion global health care company. He became Baxter's chief executive officer in January 1999 and assumed the additional responsibility of chairman of the board in January 2000.

Harry is active in business, education, and civic affairs. He serves on the board of directors of Leidos Corporation, Option Care Health, and Performance Health, and is on the board of trustees of Northwestern University, The Conference

Board, Endeavor Health System, and the Archdiocese of Chicago Finance Committee and School Board. He is a member of the Dean's Global Advisory Board of Northwestern University's Kellogg School of Management. He is a member of the Council of CEOs, the Commercial Club of Chicago, and the Economics Club of Chicago.

Harry graduated summa cum laude from Lawrence University of Wisconsin in 1977 with a bachelor's degree in mathematics and economics. He received an MBA degree in finance and accounting from Northwestern University's Kellogg School of Management in 1979.

Harry and his wife, Julie, have five children and one grandchild and live in Wilmette, Illinois.

The following organizations are featured in this book. For more information or to find out how you can support them, please visit their websites.

CHAPTER 1

Demontreville Jesuit Retreat House https://demontreviller etreat.com/
The Resurrection Project https://resurrectionproject.org/

CHAPTER 2

The Michael J. Fox Foundation for Parkinson's Research https://www.michaeljfox.org/
HIAS https://hias.org/
JCFS Chicago https://www.jcfs.org/
Partners in Health https://www.pih.org/

CHAPTER 3

One Hope https://onehopenetwork.org/
Everyone Village https://everyonevillage.org/

Berkeley Community Scholars https://berkeleyscholars.org/
Los Angeles Regional Food Bank https://www.lafood
bank.org/

CHAPTER 4

McKenzie River Trust https://mckenzieriver.org/
Kheyti https://www.kheyti.com/

CHAPTER 5

Christopher Wolf Crusade https://cwc.ngo/

CHAPTER 6

Kenyatta National Hospital Hope Hostel Project https://
knh.or.ke/index.php/ongoing/
Maziwa https://maziwabreastfeeding.com/
Macedonia2025 https://www.macedonia2025.com/
Shri Yoga https://www.shriyoga.org/

CHAPTER 7

One Acre Fund https://oneacrefund.org/

CHAPTER 8

Covenant House https://www.covenanthousebc.org/
Gallagher Foundation https://gallagherfoundation.org/

NOTES

CHAPTER 1

1. Martin Reuter, Clemens Frenzel, Nora T. Walter, Sebastian Markett, and Christian Montag, "Investigating the Genetic Basis of Altruism: The Role of the COMT Val158Met Polymorphism," *Social Cognitive and Affective Neuroscience* 6, no. 5 (October 2011): 662–668. https://doi.org/10.1093/scan/nsq083.
2. The Resurrection Project, "Our Story," 2023. Retrieved from https://resurrectionproject.org/.

CHAPTER 2

1. Amna Nawaz and Cybele Mayes-Osterman, "Surgeon General Discusses Health Risks of Loneliness and Steps to Help Connect with Others," PBS.org, May 2, 2023. Retrieved from https://www.pbs.org/newshour/show/surgeon-general-discusses-health-risks-of-loneliness-and-steps-to-help-connect-with-others#:~:text=A%20new%20report%20from%20his,Dr.
2. Michael J. Fox Foundation, Board of Directors, Bonnie Strauss. Retrieved Dec. 13, 2023, from https://www.michaeljfox.org/bio/bonnie-strauss.

3. Winston Sieck, "What Is Cultural Sensitivity and How Does It Develop?" GlobalCognition.org, Sept. 21, 2021. Retrieved from https://www.globalcognition.org/what-is-cultural-sensitivity/.

4. JCFS Chicago, "Lifting Every Neighbor," 2023. Retrieved from https://www.youtube.com/watch?v=kbpM4wMmKqo.

5. Robert Frost, "The Road Not Taken," *Poetry Foundation*, Retrieved April 23, 2024, from https://www.poetryfoundation.org/poems/44272/the-road-not-taken.

6. CDC, "Social Determinants of Health at CDC," Dec. 8, 2022. Retrieved from https://www.cdc.gov/about/sdoh/index.html.

7. Data.AustinTexas.gov, "Number and Percentage of Residents Living Below the Poverty Level (Poverty Rate)," October 2022. Retrieved from https://data.austintexas.gov/stories/s/EOA-B-1-Number-and-percentage-of-residents-living-/kgf9-tcgd/.

CHAPTER 3

1. Stephen Covey, *The 7 Habits of Highly Effective People: 30th Anniversary Edition* (Simon and Schuster, 2020).

2. Franklin Covey, "Circle of Influence," 2022. Retrieved from https://resources.franklincovey.com/mkt-7hv1/circle-of-influence.

3. City of Eugene, "Homelessness." Retrieved Dec. 21, 2023, from https://www.eugene-or.gov/3470/Homelessness.

4. Everyone Village, "Co-Creating Brave Communities of Belonging Where Everyone Can Flourish," 2024. Retrieved from https://everyonevillage.org/about-us/.

5. U.S. Department of Housing and Urban Development, "The 2022 Annual Homelessness Report to Congress," 2022. Retrieved from https://www.huduser.gov/portal/sites/default/files/pdf/2022-AHAR-Part-1.pdf.

6. Marc Freedman, "What Happens When Old and Young Connect," *Greater Good Magazine*, April 22, 2019. Retrieved from https://greatergood.berkeley.edu/article/item/what_happens_when_old_and_young_connect.

7. National Fire Protection Association, "U.S. Fire Department Profile 2020," 2022. Retrieved from https://www.nfpa.org/education-and-research/research/nfpa-research/fire-statistical-reports/us-fire-department-profile.

8. National Volunteer Fire Council, "Volunteer Fire Service Fact Sheet," 2022. Retrieved from https://www.nvfc.org/wp-content/uploads/2022/12/NVFC-Volunteer-Fire-Service-Fact-Sheet.pdf.

9. Feeding America, "Food Waste and Food Rescue," 2024. Retrieved from https://www.feedingamerica.org/our-work/reduce-food-waste.

10. Move for Hunger, "What Is Hunger?" Retrieved Jan. 26, 2024, from https://moveforhunger.org/hunger-facts.

11. Public Exchange, "Tracking Food and Nutrition Security in Los Angeles County," February 2023. Retrieved from https://publicexchange.usc.edu/wp-content/uploads/2023/02/USC-Food-Insecurity-in-LA-County_Research Brief_Feb2023.pdf.

ЄЄЄЄЄЄ

CHAPTER 4

1. Andrew Bowman, "An Audacious and Timely Conservation Challenge," Land Trust Alliance, Jan. 29, 2021. Retrieved from https://landtrustalliance.org/blog/an-audacious-and-timely-conservation-challenge.
2. Joel Barker, "The Starthrower" (inspired by the writing of Loren Eiseley). Retrieved from https://starthrower.com/pages/the-star-thrower-story.

CHAPTER 5

1. Centers for Disease Control and Prevention (CDC), "Understanding the Opioid Overdose Epidemic." Retrieved Jan. 4, 2024, from https://www.cdc.gov/opioids/basics/epidemic.html.
2. CDC, "Policy Impact: Prescription Painkiller Overdoses," 2011. Retrieved from https://www.cdc.gov/drugoverdose/pdf/policyimpact-prescriptionpainkillerod-a.pdf.
3. Johns Hopkins Medicine, "Opioids," Retrieved Feb. 4, 2024, from https://www.hopkinsmedicine.org/health/treatment-tests-and therapies/opioids#:~:text=About%2075%25%20of%20people%20in,to%20obtain%20than%20prescription%20opioids.
4. U.S. Food and Drug Administration (FDA), "Timeline of Selected FDA Activities and Significant Events Addressing Substance Use and Overdose Prevention." Retrieved Jan. 21, 2024, from https://www.fda.gov/drugs/information-drug-class/timeline-selected-fda-activities-and-significant-events-addressing-substance-use-and-overdose.
5. Joint Commission, "The Joint Commission's Pain Standards: Origins and Evolution," 2017. Retrieved from https://www.jointcommission.org/-/media/tjc/documents/resources/pain-management/pain_std_history_web_version_0512 2017pdf.

6. Cambodian Children's Fund, "New Community School Opens Near Old Dump," 2014. Retrieved from https://www.cambodianchildrensfund.org/stories-news/new-community-school-opens-near-old-dump.

7. Ronald Hirsch, "The Opioid Epidemic: It's Time to Place Blame Where It Belongs," *Missouri Medicine*, 2017. Retrieved from https://www.ncbi.nlm.nih.gov/pmc/articles/PMC6140023/.

8. American Psychiatric Association, "Nearly One in Three People Know Someone Addicted to Opioids; More than Half of Millennials Believe It Is Easy to Get Illegal Opioids," May 6, 2018. Retrieved from https://www.psychiatry.org/news-room/news-releases/nearly-one-in-three-people-know-someone-addicted-t.

9. Amazon, "The Flight, Top Reviews in the United States," Dec. 13, 2022. Retrieved from https://www.amazon.com/Flight-Cammie-Wolf-Rice/dp/1665304952/ref=sr_1_1?crid=NPO4Z7AGWC89&keywords=Cammie+Wolf+Rice+the+flight&qid=1704469537&s=books&sprefix=cammie+wolf+rice+the+flight%2Cstripbooks%2C152&sr=1-1.

10. L. Cao and J. Van Deusen, "US Medical School Curriculum on Opioid Use Disorder—A Topic Review of Current Curricular Research and Evaluation of Winning Student-Designed Opioid Curricula for the 2021 Coalition on Physician Education in Substance Use Disorders Curricular Competition," *Frontiers in Pain Research* (Lausanne), 2023. Retrieved from https://www.ncbi.nlm.nih.gov/pmc/articles/PMC10641501/pdf/fpain-04-1257141.pdf.

11. American Medical Association (AMA), "2021 Overdose Epidemic Report," 2022. Retrieved from https://www.ama-assn.org/system/files/ama-overdose-epidemic-report.pdf.

12. Sara Skoog, "Harm Reduction Award Honors Efforts to Treat Addiction," Winter 2023, *Helix.* Retrieved from https://www.rosalindfranklin.edu/helix/winter-2023/harm-reduction-award-honors-efforts-to-treat-addiction/.

13. Institute of Medicine Committee on Palliative and End-of-Life Care for Children and Their Families; M. J. Field, R. E. Behrman, eds., *When Children Die: Improving Palliative and End-of-Life Care for Children and Their Families* (National Academies Press, 2003), Appendix E. Retrieved from https://www.ncbi.nlm.nih.gov/books/NBK220798/.

14. Jodie Jacobs, "Miles for Monte Makes One Final Statement," Oct. 4, 1998, *Chicago Tribune.* Retrieved from https://www.chicagotribune.com/news/ct-xpm-1998-10-04-9810030044-story.html.

CHAPTER 6

1. Malaka Gharib, "The Pandemic Changed the World of 'Voluntourism.' Some Folks Like the New Way Better," *NPR,* Jan. 15, 2021. Retrieved from https://www.npr.org/sections/goatsandsoda/2021/07/15/1009911082/the-pandemic-changed-the-world-of-voluntourism-some-folks-like-the-new-way-bette.

2. Centers for Disease Control and Prevention (CDC), "Breastfeeding: Why It Matters." Retrieved Feb. 13, 2024, from https://www.cdc.gov/breastfeeding/about-breastfeeding/why-it-matters.html.

3. Macedonia2025, "Tribute to John Bitove Sr.," Retrieved Feb. 19, 2024, from https://www.macedonia2025.com/our-visionary-founder/.

4. Debra Black, "Giant in Food Business John Bitove Sr. Lived for Family and for the Old Country," *Toronto Star,*

July 31, 2015. Retrieved from https://www.thestar.com/news/investigations/giant-in-food-business-john-bitove-sr-lived-for-family-and-for-the-old-country/article_f3498df7-bd2d-5319-8582-cf504b0a6b5c.html.

5. United States Agency for International Development (USAID), North Macedonia, Fact Sheets, "Citizens Against Corruption," April 19, 2023. Retrieved from https://www.usaid.gov/north-macedonia/fact-sheets/apr-19-2023-citizens-against-corruption.

6. Catherine Woodyard, "Exploring the Therapeutic Effects of Yoga and Its Ability to Increase Quality of Life," *International Journal of Yoga*, 2011. Retrieved from https://www.ncbi.nlm.nih.gov/pmc/articles/PMC3193654/.

CHAPTER 7

1. D. M. Salgado Baptisa, M. Farid, D. Fayad, et al., "Climate Change and Chronic Food Insecurity in Sub-Saharan Africa," *Departmental Papers*, IMF eLibrary, 2022. Retrieved from https://www.elibrary.imf.org/view/journals/087/2022/016/article-A001-en.xml.

2. One Acre Fund, "Our Impact," 2024. Retrieved from https://oneacrefund.org/our-impact.

3. UN World Food Program USA, "What the 'Hunger Season' Means for Farmers Fighting Famine," 2021. Retrieved from https://www.wfpusa.org/articles/what-the-unger-season-means-for-farmers-fighting-famine/.

4. Ariadna Curto and Cathryn Tonne, "Kerosene-Based Lighting: An Overlooked Source of Exposure to Household Air Pollution?" *Clean Air Journal*, 2020. Retrieved from http://www.scielo.org.za/scielo.php?script=sci_arttext&pid=S2410-972X2020000100011.

5. UN Sustainable Development Goals (SDG), Goal 7. Retrieved Feb. 6, 2024, from https://sdgs.un.org/goals/goal7.

6. OneAcreFund.org, "Carving a Space for Women in a Male-Dominated Field," June 4, 2022. Retrieved from https://oneacrefund.org/articles/carving-space-women-male-dominated-field.

CHAPTER 8

1. Ingrid Phaneuf, "Cummins Says Farewell to a Legend," *Truck News*, Oct. 1, 2004. Retrieved from https://www.truck news.com/features/cummins-says-farewell-to-a-legend/.

2. City of Vancouver, "Downtown Eastside." Retrieved Feb. 29, 2024, from https://vancouver.ca/news-calendar/downtown-eastside.aspx.

3. Human Rights Watch, World Report 2023, "Turkey Events of 2022." Retrieved from https://www.hrw.org/world-report/2023/country-chapters/turkey.

4. Children Learn What They Live, Dorothy Law Nolte, Copyright 1972; free printable poem retrieved from https://storage.googleapis.com/wzukusers/user-34533481/documents/8671803a56b44b96a915cc3fd5c0 cd2f/CLWTL%20short%20w%3Aweb%20PDF.pdf.

CHAPTER 9

1. Andrew Stanley, "Global Inequalities," March 2022, International Monetary Fund. Retrieved from https://www.imf.org/en/Publications/fandd/issues/2022/03/Global-inequalities-Stanley.

2. Tom Infield, "Navigating the Challenges of the U.S. Political Landscape," Pew Research Center, Feb. 2, 2024. Retrieved from https://www.pewtrusts.org/en/trust/archive/winter-2024/navigating-the-challenges-of-the-us-political-landscape.

3. Viktor Frankl, *Man's Search for Meaning* (Beacon Press, 2006).

4. Stanford Encyclopedia of Philosophy, "Biological Altruism," published 2003; revised 2013. Retrieved from https://plato.stanford.edu/entries/altruism-biological/.

5. Corey Moss, "Pope John Paul II: Friend of Bono, Fan of Pop Culture," MTV.com, April 1, 2005. Retrieved from https://www.mtv.com/news/e68b7x/pope-john-paul-ii-friend-of-bono-fan-of-pop-culture.

6. Philip Pullela, "Bono and the Pope Harmonize on Climate Change, Girls' Education," *Reuters*, May 19, 2022. Retrieved from https://www.reuters.com/business/environment/bono-pope-harmonize-climate-change-girls-education-2022-05-19/.

7. Olivia Waxman, "The Story Behind Netflix's 'We Are the World' Documentary, *The Greatest Night in Pop*," *Time Magazine*, Jan. 29, 2024. Retrieved from https://time.com/6588802/netflix-doc-greatest-night-in-pop-we-are-the-world/.

8. CBS Chicago, "Legacy of Walter Payton Lives on with NFL Man of the Year Award," Feb. 1, 2016. Retrieved from https://www.cbsnews.com/chicago/news/legacy-of-walter-payton-lives-on-with-nfl-man-of-the-year-award/.

9. Sara Kettler, "Why Dolly Parton Has Devoted Her Life to Helping Children Read," Biography.com, April 13, 2020. Retrieved from https://www.biography.com/musicians/dolly-parton-imagination-library.

10. UNHCR, "Remarks by UNHCR Special Envoy, Ms. Angelina Jolie, on World Refugee Day," June 20, 2021. Retrieved from https://www.unhcr.org/news/press-releases/remarks-unhcr-special-envoy-ms-angelina-jolie-world-refugee-day.

11. The Borgen Project, "How the Maddow Jolie-Pitt Foundation Is Supporting Cambodia," *Borgen Magazine,* Nov. 23, 2023. Retrieved from https://www.borgenmaga zine.com/maddox-jolie-pitt-foundation/.

12. BBC News, "'I Have a Very Fortunate Life' Angelia Jolie," 2015. Retrieved from https://www.youtube.com/watch?v=lH70NQr0KEs.

13. Forbes.com, "Jackie Chan: Philanthropy's Hardest Working Man," 2011. Retrieved from https://www.forbes.com/global/2011/0718/heroes-philanthropy-11-jackie-chan-dayne-nourse-hardest-working.html?sh=5ab47c4f19eb.

14. Today, "Chan Named Goodwill Ambassador for UNICEF," 2004. Retrieved from https://www.today.com/popculture/chan-named-goodwill-ambassador-unicef-wbna4837620.

15. Minnesota Council of Churches, "About Refugees," 2024. Retrieved from https://www.mnchurches.org/what-we-do/refugee-services/about-refugees.

16. National Shrine of St. Francis of Assisi, "The Peace Prayer." Retrieved March 7, 2024, from http://www.shrinesf.org/franciscan-prayer.html.

INDEX

Activity, productivity (contrast), 27

Addiction, speaking up/
out, 104–106

Aduro Biotech, founding, 119

Altruism, 189

American Business Immigration
Coalition, 21

American Trends Panel (Pew
Research Center), 187–188

Bachmann-Strauss Dystonia &
Parkinson's Foundation
(BSDPF), 34–35

Berkeley Community
Scholars, 61–64
life trajectory, 63
mission, 61–62

Biological altruism, 189

Bitove, Jr., John, 130, 132

Bitove, Sr., John, 130, 131

Blazhevski, Nikica
Mojsoska, 133–134

Boğaziçi University, 176

Bologna, Alison, 37, 135–138

Bono, humanitarian
efforts, 192–193

Borders, bridges (building), 191

Briner, Monte, 115

Brock, Peter, 64

Buss, Patti, 50, 53

Buss, Steve, 54–55

Butterfly effect, 201–202

Cambodian Children's Fund
(CCF), 103

Career, progression, 11

Chan, Jackie (UNICEF
Ambassador), 200

Charity, support (donor demon-
stration), 50

"Children Learn What They Live"
(Law Nolte), 184

Choices, 25–26, 41–43

Christopher Wolf Crusade,
99–100, 101
energy, 107
funding, absence (impact), 111
ground, breaking, 110
journey, 113–114
life care specialists, introduction, 113
partnership, 112
positive change, 116
work, expansion, 108

Church, involvement, 11

Circle of influence, 51, 71–72

Clark, Harrison Thomas
(photo), 205

Collier, Tony, 70

Commins, Pat, 58

Community, 25–26, 36–41
  assistance, 59
  barriers, breakdown, 167–171
  bridges, building, 191
  building, 16
  embracing, 37–38
  interaction, 22
  members, self-interests
    (bridging), 20
  support, 98
  transformation/
    strengthening, 22
  trouble, 19–20
  volunteering, 17–21
  vulnerability, 41–42
Community Breastfeeding
  Ambassadors (Maziwa),
  impact, 127–128
Connections, 25–26, 32–36
Connections, community, and
  choices (three Cs), 25–26
  reflections, 46
Conover, Shoshanah, 39
Continuum, 3–4
Conversation, impact, 9
Corruption, elimination, 132–133
Cottages of Hope, 53, 55
  volunteer construction, 56
Covenant House, 170
  expansion, 169–170
Covey, Stephen, 51
COVID, impact/shutdown, 88,
  95, 138–139
Crop failure, impact, 150
Cultural sensitivity, definition, 38
Cummins Engine Foundation,
  founding, 167

Demontreville Jesuit Retreat
  House, participation, 30–31
Deportation, risk, 191
Dollywood Foundation, 197–198

Earthshot Prize, The, 90–091
Economies of scale, 128
Emotional crossroads, 104
Empowerment, 50–51
Endeavor Health (NorthShore
  University Health
  System), 171–172
Everyone Village, structures
  (building/installation),
  53, 55
Existential question, 95
Experiences, sharing, 12

Faith, importance, 13
Family
  foundation, 166
    establishment, 167–168
  support, 69
Farmer, Paul, 41–43
"Farmers First" (One Acre man-
  tra), 151–152, 160
Fentanyl, usage/overdose, 104
Financial security, building, 20
Finn Rock Reach, volunteer
  work, 84–85
Firefighters, volunteering, 65–68
Firehall No. 5 project, 170
  funding, 169–170
Flight: My Opioid Journey (Wolf
  Rice), 105
Flood, Michael, 69–71, 73–74
Food
  deserts, 73
  drive, donation, 73–74
  importance, 79–80
  insecurity, 72
Food banks
  circle of influence, 71–72
  resource redistribution, 70–71
  staples, 72–73
Fox, Michael J., 34
Frankl, Viktor, 188

Fulfillment, sense, 85
Future, creation, 143

Gallagher, Ellen, 171–174, 178
  photo, 180
Gallagher Foundation, 171–184
  formation, 174–175
  future, 182–184
  Global Leadership
    Summit, 179–180
  photo, 180
  leadership capabilities, build-
    ing, 171–172
  scholars, 175, 181–183
Gallagher, Jerry, 172–182
  photo, 172
Gallagher, Megan, 175–183
Gallagher Prindiville,
  Megan, 175–177
Gallagher Scholars (Gallagher
  Graduate Scholars), 178–179,
  181–182
Gates Foundation, seed
  capital, 127
Genuine humility, 197–198
Gifts, sharing, 60–61
Global footprint, 145,
  154, 161–162
Global Leadership Summit
  (Gallagher
  Foundation), 179–180
  photo, 180
Global recognition, 90–91
Global thinking, 81–83
Golden Rule, 141
Goward, Elizabeth, 5, 80–81, 83–85
GPF Foundation, collaboration,
  107
Graduate Advisory Council, 183
Grady Memorial Hospital, 107, 108
  pilot program, success,
    111, 112–113

Graham, William, 61
Grassroots, 90–91
  big idea, 91–97
  growth, 77, 97–98
  roles, 83
"Greatest Night in Pop, The"
  (documentary), 194–195
Grebein, Donald, 138
Green Island, 77
  long-term plans, 78
  volunteers, 82
  "Watershed Wednesday," 81
Grehan, Farrell, 206

Habitat for Humanity, 175
Happiness, impact, 15
Head Start, 201
HIAS Immigration &
  Citizenship, 38–39
History, learning, 8
HIV/AIDS patients,
  interaction, 93
Honesty/respect, treatment, 7
Hope Hostel (Kenyatta National
  Hospital), building
  (support), 123–124
Hosting, 16
Humanitarian efforts, 192–193
Hunger season, 150

Imagination Library (Parton), 198
Immigrants, hardship/
  prejudice, 16
Immigration services,
  passion, 21
Incubators, solar power
  (providing), 94–95
Influence, 6–15
  circle of influence, 51, 71–72
  link, 13
  uncovering, 22–23
Influence, continuation, 5–6

Intergenerational
relationships, 60
Isaacs, Stephen, 4, 61,
95–96, 119–125
curiosity/motivation, 121–122
transition, 122
volunteering (photo), 120

Jackie Chan Charitable
Foundation, formation, 200
Jacobs, Donald, 12, 61
Jamal, Sahar, 125–128
Jansen, Bill, 14–15
JCFS Chicago, video, 40
Jim Yong Kim, meeting, 41–42
Jolie, Angelina, 198–200
refugee work, 201

Karma yoga, 136
Kasigau, Isaacs commitment, 124
Kheyti, 79, 85–91
approach, 151
grassroots endeavor, 89–90
greenhouses, usage, 88–89
mission, evolution, 87
solution, making, 88–90
Kindness, act, 50
Kraemer family (photo), 7
Kraemer, Daniel, 59–60
Kraemer, Jr., Harry M. Jansen
(photo), 8
Kraemer, Julie, 11, 13, 60
Kraemer, Sr., Harry, 10, 206
photo, 9

Land Trust Alliance, 80
Land, trust perpetuity holding, 81
Larson, Anita, 97–98
Last Mile Health, volunteering, 43
Latin America Student
Organization (LASO), 18
Law Nolte, Dorothy, 184

Leaders, defining, 31
Leadership journey, 13–14
Lee, David, 5
Lee, Howard/Ruby, 44
Lee, Patrick, 5, 41–46
Legacy, 73–74, 99
building, 13, 29, 32,
184–185, 201
consideration, 15
creation, 140, 165
cycle, continuation, 165
definition, 3
establishment, 79–80, 166
exploration, 3–4
foundation, 22–23
impact, 69
lasting legacy, 114–116
living, 13, 29
nurture/nature, relationship, 4
phases, 188
power, 16
self-reflection, impact, 26–27
Life care specialist, role, 110–113
Life lessons, 7
Light, Jane, 38–39
Little Village (La Villita), problems, 19–20
Living river, 83–85
Living Water Family
Fellowship, 54
Local actions, 81–83
Local leaders, legacy, 155
LoManto, Nick, 65–68
Los Angeles Regional Food
Bank, 69–74
program, evolution, 72–73
Lugari District, 158–159
Luminaries, impact, 195–200

Macedonia2025, 129–135
country, rebranding, 133–135
legacy, 132, 134–135

"One Vision for Accelerated
Growth," 133
values-based leadership,
131–133
Maddox Jolie-Pitt Foundation,
activities, 199
Madison Dearborn portfolio, 35
Malawi
solar project, failure, 94
yellow quail, protection, 91–97
Material possessions, 11
Maziwa
mothers/babies, assistance, 125
Sahar establishment, 126
sales, doubling, 127–128
McKenzie River Trust, 77, 97
drinking water protection, 79
events, 83
fieldwork, 78
land/water protection, 80–85
practices, adoption, 84
volunteers, 78
"Watershed Wednesday," 81
Mentees, confidence
(bolstering), 64
Mercer University School of
Medicine, partnership, 112
Michael J. Fox Foundation for
Parkinson's Research, 34–36
Miller, Irwin, 167
Minnesota Council of Churches,
refugee activity, 201
MIT SOLVE, seed capital, 127
Morrison, Daven, 28–29, 115–116
Muench, Beverly, 167–169, 173
Muench, Gottfried "Guff,"
167–169, 173
Muench, Peter, 169
Multinational NGOs, impact, 149
Multiplier effect, 49–50
Murthy, Vivek, 28
Music, love, 192–193

Narrative, initiation, 21
National Volunteer Fire Council,
volunteer firefighters
(importance), 68
Nature/nurture, 188–192
Nonprofit organizations, board
(serving), 12–13
Nonprofit social enterprise,
scaling, 118–119
Northern Frontier District
(Kenya), 123
Northshore University Health
System, expansion, 13

One Acre Fund, 6–7, 89, 145–147
farmer (photo), 151
"Farmers First" mantra,
151–152, 160
harvest/yield, 156–157
inspiration, 148–149
legacy, measurement, 146
local leaders, legacy, 155
mission, 150, 160
partnership, 154
seeds, usage, 162–163
success, 150–151
support, 120–121, 158
training, 156, 158
world, changing, 153–154
One Hope, 50, 52–61
volunteers, 53, 56
"One Vision for Accelerated
Growth" (Macedonia2025
document), 133
Open-mindedness, 92
Opioid addiction, 104–106
fact-finding mission, 106
life care specialist, role,
110–113
prevention/treatment pro-
grams, stigma (barrier), 105
speaking up/out, 104–106

Opioid crisis, traction, 109
Others
  giving, 59–60
  light, following, 200–201
Others, helping (importance), 11
"Overdose Epidemic Report"
    (American Medical
    Association), 106–107
OxyContin, problems, 102–103

Pacific Spirt Foundation,
    167–171
  generations, impact, 170–171
  giving/projects, 169–170
  mission statement, 168
  projects, 169–170
Pain, expectations (setting), 109
Partners in Health, 41–45
Parton, Dolly Rebecca, 197–198
  literacy/education work, 201
Past, understanding
    (importance), 8
Payton, Walter *(Sweetness)*,
    196–197
Peace Corps volunteer, role, 93
Personal passions, 74–75
Philanthropic project/organiza-
    tion, 28–29
Piechowicz, Gabe, 55
Pillars, 132–133
Political voice, absence,
    191–192
Pope John Paul II, Bono
    meeting, 193
Present, celebration, 47
Pritzker, J.B., 21
Profit-and-loss statement, 14
Project Hope (One Hope out-
    reach), 52–53
Public policy, study, 19
Purpose
  confirmation, 191
  identification, 31

"Question-and-opinion" dis-
    cussions, 61
Questions, broadness/
    application, 30

Racist/segregationist policies,
    systemic imbalance (cor-
    rection), 174
Raymundo, Raul, 16–22
Rebranding, 134
Resurrection Project, The, 17, 19
  launch, 20
  seed capital, leverage, 20–21
Rice Academy, The, 103
Rice, John, 102–104, 106–107,
    113
Richie, Lionel, 194–195
Rise Fund, 193
Robinhold, Dan, 81–82
Rockefeller Foundation, establish-
    ment, 165–166
Rockefeller, Jr., John D., 165
Rockefeller, Sr., John D., 165
Role models, 44–46
Rwanda, One Acre Fund
    (impact), 153–154

Saumya (investment
    banker), 90–91
  farmer issues/challenges, 87
  first failure, 86
  impact, 85–86
Schenker, Mara, 107
  Christoper Wolf Crusade
    champion, 108–110
Self-reflection, 25, 141
  benefits, 27
  decisions, 41
  depth, 66–67
  engagement, 29
  importance, 190
  life/legacy tool, 26–29
  practice, 190

time allotment, 27–28
  absence, 33–34
  timing/location, 29–32
Sheds of Hope, 54
Shri Bark, 139
Shri Studio, 135–140
  opening, 37
  service, 140
  student service, 136
Shri Yoga
  outreach model, 139
  values, display, 137
Sikhakhane, Zipho, 180
Silent retreat, attendance, 30
Skills, building, 176
Small, significance, 49
Small things, impact, 57–59
Smith, Sherry, 62–64
Social enterprise, impact, 86
Social justice legacy, 38–39
Stewardship
  grand plan, 97–98
  humility, 84
Stories, learning, 5–6
Strauss, Tom/Bonnie, connection/
  passion, 32–36
Strauss, Tom (marathon), comple-
  tion (photo), 35
Students, support (provid-
  ing), 62–63
Sub-Saharan Africa, droughts/
  cyclones (projection), 146
Success, 190
  defining, 160–161
  guarantee, absence, 79
"Support, honor, respect,
  inspire," 135, 138
Systemic injustices, addressing, 19

Team member, skills/expe-
  riences, 39
Temple Sholom, social justice
  legacy, 38–40

Thoreau, Henry David, 193
Those guys, gender-
  neutral term, 117
Tisatayane, Mathews, 92–97
  solar project, failure, 94
Trajkovski, Boris, 129–130
Trust, building, 93

Umodzi Poultry, 92–97
  quail chick, 91
  success, 96
  total sales, pledge, 96–97
United Nations High
  Commissioner for
  Refugees (UNHCR),
  198–200
United States Agency for
  International
  Development (2023
  report), 132–133
UN Sustainable Development
  Goals (SDGs)
  needs, 152–153
  support, 193
US presidential election (2024),
  political environment,
  187–188

Values-based leader, 12, 117
Values-based legacy, 28
Values-based life, 29
Values, identification, 31
Volunteers
  extension, 39
  firefighters, importance, 68
  retirees, involvement, 81–82
  staffing, 67–68
Voluntourism, problems, 122

Walter and Connie Payton
  Foundation, 196–197
Walter Payton Liver Center,
  opening, 197

Wanjala, Pauline, 146, 155–162
  career journey, 159–160
  promotion, 157–159
  responsibilities, increase, 158
  success, defining, 160–161
Water, importance, 79–80
Watts, Wayne, 60
"We Are the World," 194–195
WiMAX broadband
    (Motorola), 130
Wolf, Christopher
  crusade, 101–114
  death, 99–100
  photo, 100
Wolf Rice, Cammie, 101, 103–105,
    109, 113

photo, 100
support, 110–111
World Food Program USA, lean
    season, 150
World, polarization, 187
Wraparound services,
    providing, 55

Yemaachi Biotech, 119
Youn, Andrew, 147–155
Youn Impact Scholars, 147
Your 168 (Kraemer), 27–28

Zafirovski, Mike, 36, 129–135

OTHER BOOKS FROM

HARRY KRAEMER

BECOMING THE BEST

FROM THE BESTSELLING AUTHOR OF *FROM VALUES TO ACTION*

BUILD A WORLD-CLASS ORGANIZATION THROUGH **VALUES-BASED LEADERSHIP**

HARRY M. JANS

Becoming The Best
ISBN: 978-1-118-99942-4

"Values and culture are paramount to corporate leadership. This book provides leaders with the tools to develop their talent."
—**JEFF IMMELT**, chairman and CEO, General Electric Company

FROM VALUES TO ACTION

THE FOUR PRINCIPLES OF **VALUES-BASED LEADERSHIP**

HARRY M. JANSEN KRAEMER Jr.

From Values to Action
ISBN: 978-0-470-88125-5

"For anyone who seeks to lead a values-based life, *Your 168* is a personal and inspiring guide to making the most of what matters."
ALAN MULALLY,
Retired CEO of Ford Motor Company and Boeing Commercial Airplanes

MAKE **EVERY HOUR** OF YOUR WEEK COUNT

YOUR 168

FINDING PURPOSE AND SATISFACTION IN A **VALUES-BASED LIFE**

HARRY M. JANSEN KRAEMER, JR.

WILEY

Your 168
ISBN: 978-1-119-65854-2

WILEY